DEAR MR. YOU

Mary-Louise Parker

SCRIBNER

New York   London   Toronto   Sydney   New Delhi

Scribner
An Imprint of Simon & Schuster, Inc.
1230 Avenue of the Americas
New York, NY 10020

First Scribner hardcover edition November 2015

For information about special discounts for bulk purchases,
please contact Simon & Schuster Special Sales at 1-866-506-1949
or business@simonandschuster.com.

The Simon & Schuster Speakers Bureau can bring authors to your
live event. For more information or to book an event, contact the
Simon & Schuster Speakers Bureau at 1-866-248-3049 or visit our website
at www.simonspeakers.com.

Manufactured in the United States of America

10 9 8 7 6 5 4 3 2 1

Library of Congress Cataloging-in-Publication Data

Parker, Mary-Louise.
  Dear Mr. You / Mary-Louise Parker.
    pages cm
  1. Parker, Mary-Louise. 2. Parker, Mary-Louise—Relations with men.
3. Parker, Mary-Louise—Family. 4. Parker, Mary-Louise—Friends and
associates. 5. Actors—United States—Biography. I. Title.
  PN2287.P267A3 2015
  791.4302'8092—dc23   2015017170

ISBN 978-1-5011-0783-2
ISBN 978-1-5011-0785-6 (ebook)

"Dear Daddy" and "Dear Mr. You" appeared in somewhat altered versions titled "My
Dad, My Boy" and "If You're Good You Get Dessert" in the June/July 2012, volume
157, nos. 6 and 7, and the August 2009, volume 152, no. 2 issues of *Esquire*, respectively.

For my mother

Contents

DEAR
MR. YOU

Dear Mr. You,

Manly creature, who smells good even when you don't, you wake up too slowly, with fuzzy, vertical hair and a slightly lost look on your face as though you are seven or seventy-five; to you, because you can notice a woman with a healthy chunk of years or pounds on her and let out a wolf whistle under your breath and mean it; because you thought either rug would be fine, really it would; to you who can fix my screen door, my attitude, and open most jars; to you who codifies, slams a puck, builds a decent cabinet or the perfect sandwich; to you who gave a twenty to the kids selling Hershey bars and waited three hours for me at baggage claim in your flannel shirt; you, sir, you took my order, my pulse, my bullshit; to you, boy grown up, the gentleman, soldier, professor, or caveman; to you and to that guy at the concession stand; thank you for lying on the hood of that car and watching stars plummet, thank you for the tour of the elevator cage, the sound booth, the alley; thank you for the kaleidoscope, the get-well tequila, the painting, the truth; thank you for the brown diamonds and blue points; to you, who carried me across the parking lot, to the ER, and up the stairs; to you who shows up every so often only to confuse and torment, and you who stays in orbit to my left and steady, you stood up for me, I won't forget that; to the one who can't figure it out and never will, and to the one who lost the remote, the dog, or your way altogether. To you who I've tried to understand, so necessary and violent; you who transported, comforted, and devastated, sometimes all at once; I still have what you said was mine, I kept that, along with the memories, despite "memories" being a word I loathe for both its icky tone and wistful graveyard implications, but there it is and here I am recounting them. Some I may get wrong and others I'd love to expel forever, but thank you for them nonetheless, and this,

this is for you, Cerberus, sweet beast with your many faces, and you, Father Bob,

to the Deer Dancer because he saw me over there,

to the painter, and the poet,

to NASA, and to that cabdriver, what can I say but that I was wrong and I'm sorry,

to sweet Blue and kind Abe,

to firefighters all, especially that one,

to Uncle, and the newspaper boy and the goats,

to Little Owl, what an honor to watch your first flight,

to Rafiki Yangu, and to my mentor, and my doctor,

to the ones I never met and the ones I often wish I hadn't.

Most of all to you, Daddy. That's you in me, the far-off gaze. The poems are you, as are the good deeds and the jars of candy I hide everywhere. You are what makes me indomitable and how I know to keep walking when I feel crippled in every conceivable way. Thank you to the actual heavens and after that, and you others who make up my tremendous et cetera, this is

to you.

Dear Grandpa,

The world is at war again. That's twice now, in your lifetime.

Your only son has been overseas for eleven months. The last you heard, he and his fellow soldiers were going to make a beachhead landing on the shores of the Philippines. If your boy John was involved you can bet it went off like gangbusters. He is nineteen years old and remarkably good at life.

If there were a way to spy on him at this moment you'd see a young man wrapped inside an army-issue poncho and sleeping in the corner of a rice paddy. Artillery is firing across the road but that sound is lost in the rain, which falls in thick black sheets, and your boy sleeps long enough for that rain to surround and lift him. When he wakes he is floating on his back.

He will hit the double decades in two and a half weeks and you have a plan that's been brewing.

You go to the only bakery you know, which is two towns over. The woman behind the counter is wiping her eyes on her apron by the time you ask to buy the biggest loaf of rye bread she has. She's just gotten an earful about your son and refuses to charge you for the bread, also throwing in a few cinnamon buns. You thank her up and down and tell her you enjoy the way her blouse matches her eyes.

You have a bottle of gin for the drive back but you run out of it around the same time you run out of fuel and have to pull over to the side of the road. You hitch a ride back to the house with a nice fellow, a miner like yourself, and tell him about your plan for your son's birthday. You are open to strangers. Aside from that it's a darn good plan.

In forty-three years, your granddaughter will be found hitchhiking by the side of the road near San Francisco. She will stand there with two young men who'll encourage her to hike up her skirt and look as winsome as possible by the off-ramp. They will have constructed a sign out of cardboard to catch the eye of someone nice enough to pull over. The sign will say MARIN, PLEASE, WE'VE READ SARTRE. They'll get a ride fairly quickly from a fellow who sees only a girl with a sign, but when he stops the two boys will come running out from behind a bush. The boys will stuff themselves in that tiny car and thank the man for his generosity before he can protest.

In an hour or so your granddaughter will enter a coffee shop with one of the boys. They will have empty stomachs and less than two dollars between them. They have a plan though. The girl goes off to a corner table by herself while the boy scans the joint for someone to beat at poker. She will eat breakfast slowly, setting down her book in between bites of croissant with strawberry jam, only ordering a hot chocolate when the boy gives her the signal that he is winning and they will be able to pay for their food. A man will notice her and attempt to sit across from her, but she will give him a blank stare as she points to the boy, who has seen the man approaching. The boy will narrow his eyes and give him the universal signal for SCRAM, and as the man skulks away she will go back to her book, which is, incidentally, *The Age of Reason* by Jean-Paul Sartre. It will start to rain as the group drives across the Golden Gate Bridge. Your granddaughter loves the rain as you do, the grandfather she'll never meet. By the time she's born you are dead and your wife has married your brother. Your granddaughter never thought much about the fact that instead of "Grandma and Grandpa," it was always "Grandma and Uncle George." When she gets older she'll wish she'd met you, as you are the subject of many stories that are told and retold within the family.

It's better that you know none of this now though, as you return home and head to the kitchen. You get a handful of crackers from the bread tin to eat with liverwurst before you set about your business. You put the loaf of bread on the counter and look at it for a moment. This makes you smile. The sight of the bread, and your own cleverness; they almost make your eyes wet.

You slice the bread through the middle and dig out the guts down to the crust. Picking out the innards, you ball them up in your hand and stash that fist-bread in the icebox for your wife to come across. She may need them as meatloaf filler if she's short some beef. You are always thinking of others.

You take the bottle of hard Kentucky whiskey from its bag and admire the label, which is blurry. You nearly fall off the kitchen stool trying to read it. A sip of moonshine from a jar in the icebox feels like a swell idea. You stand with your hand on the refrigerator door and sway, letting the cold out.

The candle is a problem. You have a heck of a time finding one and have to wake your wife, who swears at you. When you say it's for the boy's birthday, she walks to the neighbors' in her housedress to ask for one. You admire her attack on life, as you watch her heading back up the driveway with a candle stub, highly perturbed. You get a kick out of the whole exercise.

The candle drips wax around the bottle top and creates a seal to protect the whiskey. You lay the sacrificial bottle in the crust coffin, for the second time thanking the powers that be for making you so goddamned ingenious. Splashing Worcestershire in the remains of the frosting creates a tinted batch with which to spell "Happy Birthday John!" The exclamation point looks like a tadpole but that adds mystery. You chuckle as you wrap it up.

When your boy sees a box with his name on it, he tears it open for any sign of home. He'd been digging foxholes to wait out the night when the first load of mail in weeks reached him by way of New Guinea. The sound of his name being called to receive a package is almost gift enough.

He digs through the newspaper and finds your cake, by now pitiful and moldy. It's bald in patches where the icing has rubbed off, but it's from you so he knows to look beneath the surface for the joke. He unties the twine around the bread and looks inside, letting go a belly laugh and waving his hand up to the sky. The other soldiers slap him on the back and wish him happy birthday while eyeing the bottle's throat like the slope of a woman's neck they could grasp with their muddy frozen hands.

John says a toast to you before passing it around and everyone joins in on the "hip-hip hooray!" The irony of celebrating is lost on those young men who are swimming in mud and sharing a tin of sardines for dinner. They raise up their rifles and fists to the skies, believing they won't have their last drink in the middle of this paddy. There will be real parties waiting back home and a chance for a fella to put on a clean shirt and tie, hear the ice clink in a decent glass of gin. The day when this is the story told while sitting in a real chair.

For now they let out their best cheer. It doesn't rouse you from where you lie facedown on the rug in West Virginia, talking to a son lost too deep in the jungle to hear you. You wonder if they have the same locusts in that part of the world where your boy is now. Locusts. You are fond of the sound but they ruin discovery. The way they rise and fall in the same exact patterns every night tells you what time it is before you get a chance to peek out a window for yourself, see where the moon ended up tacked to the sky.

Dear Daddy,

I don't know his name or rank. He must be dead now.

It was the Philippines, 1944. Your battalion was trying to divide the Japanese so they couldn't push the Americans down to the beaches. Wipe them out by the ocean, where their bodies could feed the big fish. Their bones would wash up with photos of their girls from back home floating past. The boots would be gone. During combat, soldiers take boots off the casualties, you told me, since in war all you do is walk.

This soldier saw you struggling. You couldn't recall his name, which means the gunshot in your leg was brutal, because you remembered everything. He lost his place in line to find a branch and tied the stick to your leg to get you going again, using your rifle for a cane. You fell back in, began to muscle your way through the thicket. When the pain started to set your guts on fire you slowed but didn't quit. In the jungle, night is so black you can't see your hand in front of your face but you could hear the screams of men being bayoneted fifty meters away. The guys at the back of the line were the ones getting picked off first, their bloodlines ending in the brush in the middle of an island they'd never heard of a week ago. Last was not the place to be.

The commander ordered a brief stop so the soldiers could rest. Not sleep, but have water or stare impassively at their wounds and one another. Smoke. As the hundreds of soldiers sat, you kept walking until your back of the line became the middle. Dragging your leg, you were the only one walking until you'd blown all the way to the front with a bullet in your thigh. When the commander ordered everyone up they began to pass you again, pushing you to the rear until another stop was called, but you limped through that break too. You dragged yourself by soldiers sitting on their helmets chewing tobacco, sharing a pack of Life Savers. Some had their heads in their hands while standing otherwise at attention. They were arrested in space with nowhere to go, looking like the statues that would one day represent them in public spaces, with plaques describing this battle and their bravery.

This went on an entire day longer, with you managing to hold the middle by not accepting the back. Your hand was melded to your rifle and aching like the dickens but you heaved onward, kept not taking that break. At some point when you still hadn't died, trees cleared and there was legitimate light. You were medevaced out, only to be back in combat a month later with your first Purple Heart, which you said you never understood. You'd ask, "Why do they give you a medal for being dumb enough to get shot?"

Months later, you were shivering under a blanket in Manila, thinking about getting home in time to call that girl about a date for New Year's. You hadn't stopped thinking about her since that day at the bank. She'd floated over with a note from some other gal. Her eyes were so brown. She had skin that looked like a bowl of fruit with cream painted on top, and seemed as though she might stick by a man, but quietly, with a little orchestra of sighs and run-on sentences. You asked someone what her story was. Apparently she was going to Averett College in the fall, and you remembered that while you were sitting by that campfire in the middle of war a year later. You wrote her a letter by the light of that fire, on the top of the page scrawling the words *FROM SOMEWHERE IN THE PHILIPPINES*.

Thirty years later, my teen European-tour-to-meet-boys fell through when my friend's parents said no. I was devastated and you couldn't bear it. You sold or mortgaged something and booked a family Euro-tour—not my dream, but you were so happy to give me this trip you couldn't afford that I acted excited, hoping there would be a boy on a train who would not know English and kiss me, but there were no cute boys. There was only a man on a pier in Monte Carlo who thought I was a prostitute, but the trip had moments. You and I woke early in Amsterdam to go to the diamond factory to get Mom a ring. Once there, you pushed me ("Pick one for you and your sister, please, I want you to"), so I picked the smallest, praying it was also the cheapest, but you insisted on a bigger one. We took a boat back to the hotel and I remember your face looking out over the water. I could see all the weight on you. You were dreaming and planning, brimming with if-onlys.

Going up Sixth Avenue in a taxi, your grandson said, "Mommy, aren't there so many amazing things in the world? Aren't we so lucky to be alive?" That's you in him, Daddy. He's so like you, full of extremes and heavy on the dream space. Both kids put their fists up for each other and I know that would make you happy. I try to teach them pacifism but sometimes it's only halfhearted. "Lady, this outfit you are running here is a bunch of bull," you said to that librarian who accused me of lying about how many books I'd read. "Mean lady, you are the f word," Will said to the woman in the dog park who called me stupid for leaving the gate open.

My children may never see me hunched over a checkbook and sense my mounting panic, or come home late and find me in the street armed with a shovel as I take the driver of a car by the neck when liquor is smelled on him. They will watch me make much of their victories and hold a grudge until my last breath if someone treats them cruelly. This is your family I am running here. I can't take credit for more than remembering to point to you when I do something right and for continuing to put one foot in front of the other when I lose heart.

We all miss you something fierce, those of us who wouldn't exist had you not kept walking when an ordinary person would have fallen to his knees. To convey in any existing language how I miss you isn't possible. It would be like blue trying to describe the ocean.

Dear Yaqui Indian Boy,

Where did you go?

Did you fly away and leave the barrio? Most Yaqui Indians never move away. Hard life had pushed your people to the ghetto of that ghetto where I went so many days after school. I learned your streets from the window of a lowrider, the hydraulics making the car hump the pavement while we listened to Earth, Wind and Fire or the Sugarhill Gang. You must have heard us as we rode by, with Gloria and Alicia shouting, "HOTEL! MOTEL! WHAT YOU GONNA DO TODAY? (SAY WHAT?)" Arturo would drive us. He'd poke Sammy Z in the ribs and say, *ai, chécalo, look at those.* He'd point to the girls' asses bobbing up and back to the music while they stuck their heads out the window. The boys had their hair greased back and their chinos on, and the girls shellacked their feathered hair so hard with, like, a half bottle of Final Net each, they said. It would blow up from the wind in two flat pieces like horns, and their jeans? Homegirl could work some camel toe. They knew they were foxy. Those asses would never be so titanic again in their lives, you could serve a whole flan off those *culos* and it wouldn't even jiggle. My friend and I would sit between the other girls, embarrassed but thrilled, whispering about Sammy Z while mouthing to each other, *Órale vato! Que barrio!*, but not loud enough for anyone to hear us.

What did you do, Yaqui boy? Did you do like Sammy and most of the Mexican boys, marry the girl you took to prom? In Guadalupe everyone had a place. The Yaqui Indians, your people, had their space farther out. I wouldn't have seen you before and I don't even know where you went to school. My one good friend when I was fifteen was Mexican and she brought me to your hood. In the overly white community where I lived, all was murderously medium. It was hard to locate yourself there, where everything was a moderate version of something that didn't dare reach too far up or dip beneath the middle. I went to the barrio instead, trailed along to every Posada and *quinceañera*; anywhere there were empanadas and mariachis that ended their sets with "Sabor a Mi." You would never have come to my street where every boy was a football star and every girl a popular cheerleader. I hated them while sometimes wishing I was one too, a girl who was invited to dances, walked home, or occasionally felt up by a creepy uncle.

I was never noticed in my fifteenth year except by you, deer dancer. It was your Pascala and my Easter. I walked through Guadalupe to the far field, where white girls whispered that Mexicans took victims and tied them up with phone cords to rape them. That didn't scare me half as much as walking the halls at school and I didn't believe them anyway. I was the only white person for miles and *blanca* I was pale as notebook paper without the lines. I noticed the houses getting smaller and the yards more chaotic, overrun with broken cars and swing sets that served as laundry lines. We started to see more of your people as they walked to their Easter, the big holy day. Soon there was just the smell of dough frying and clusters of people, some in costume. My friend headed for the biggest group, packed so tightly that we couldn't see what they were looking at. Flashing her brilliant smile at a neighbor, she grabbed my hand and he made space for us so we could slip in front.

You were there. There was an old man feet away from you, playing a drum made out of a gourd floating in water. Someone was singing in Yaqui, that language so heavy on article and air, its sounds so untenably painful that every note was someone begging or losing. The music was only background though, because I was watching you. My friend whispered

The drum is the deer's heart, floating, and the sticks they play are the breath in his body

I don't know how long it took for you to hypnotize me into reverie. Before the crowd parted I'd seen your antlers above the people and part of me had worried, oh God, not an animal sacrifice, I am an Episcopalian after all, I can only jive with so much, but it wasn't. It was you, sacred, beautiful boy. You were dancing with a full shed of antlers on your head while your audience stood rapt and reverent.

By legend the deer dancer has to be summoned to dance, receiving the invitation in his sleep. It's a calling in your culture, where grave decisions are made based on dreams and flowers. Photographing a deer dancer was not allowed and signs of warning were posted. For those who believe, the dance is a fortification so strong that it purifies just to watch it, and since you don't know how many dances you will see in your lifetime, you should see every one you can. You were my one and despite your shaggy black hair and dirty face you felt as much a deer as any I've seen disappearing into the trees. Though probably my age, you'd had more thrown at you and lived harder. Your lower body was so thoroughly covered in red earth that it seemed you'd been left in the sun to rust.

I moved a half step closer, and sensed something more than saw it. A question loomed and the answer couldn't possibly be yes to *does he see me* but it was. I could feel myself being seen, though you weren't looking at me as much as dancing at me, finding me from some radar at the tip of your antlers while arching in my direction. You'd caught my frequency from where I stood at the edge of the crowd, trembling. Your chest was brown enough to make that dirt look like a softer shade of chalk as your breath made your ribs appear and recede. My pulse quickened when your deer raised up as if tracking a mate nearby. Your body was equal parts human and animal; it made me feel safe and hunted in the best way. I wanted to pet you and feed you, I wanted you to chase me and take me with your teeth. I wished you could turn my legs that red dirt color by pinning me to the ground underneath you.

Too abruptly the singing stopped. For a moment you were frozen so still that I began to doubt you'd ever actually moved. When you finally relaxed, you bent over with your hands on your knees, coming back. One of the musicians gave you a handful of

cigarettes and some of the men reached for them in exchange for
a small tip as a sign of respect. Looking around almost wearily,
you ignored them and didn't stop. Instead you walked across that
circle and closed it. You aimed straight in my direction. I stayed
fixed on you, your brown eyes, your mouth as you advanced to
me, who'd never had a boy walk to her before. Not in that way,
to choose her. The last few steps of your approach, with all the
men trailing behind, your face was square on and meeting mine at
its most open. Taller than I realized, you gazed down as my legs
shook, my arms all goose flesh with you only a deer's distance
away. We stared into each other until you held up a cigarette and
said

Quieres?

I shook my head no. You shrugged. I offered a smile, really
more than I'd ever willingly given any boy. You smiled back and
sighed quietly, turning and walking sideways for a few steps to
not close off from me, I thought. A quick last glance and you were
off, walking alongside the *Fariseos* as they pelted you with flowers.

There are relatively few of your tribe left, do you count each
other? They sold your people for twenty-five or fifty centavos a
head, you were hunted like the deer but no one talks about this.
No one knows you. Where I grew up your people lived and still
live, not far from the desert where those deer run wild, most of
those animals not living longer than four years. Mountain lions,
men with archery kits bought online, there are too many hunters
for deer to live out their potential life span. Their greatest down-

fall is mating season. That's when a buck grows careless, letting go of those eyes in the back of his head. If he gets that twitch, hoping a mate is nearby, he will turn right toward that trace of something, suddenly dreamy and reckless. That hope can lead him straight into a bullet; desire then becoming just another hard way for a deer to fall.

Dear Risk Taker,

I remember staring at the Avedon poster of the Beatles when I was four and a half. *Years old.* It was taped to the wall behind my sister's bed and I would bore holes in it, staring at them while she played their records, which I already knew. When I was seven or so I was putting on a play in my backyard for an audience of zero, called "Imposter Beatles." My character was a girl named Sweetie who was seduced by four men claiming to be John, Paul, George, and Ringo. Sometimes the girl down the block joined in but usually I enacted the whole thing alone or with my dog. The beginning was a montage where Sweetie received compliments from Paul about her personality and halter dress, followed by a section where she played on the swings while they serenaded her with songs from *Revolver*. At some point she began to tap into clues that these were imposters with a plot to kidnap her. Some days Sweetie was gagged and handcuffed by the Faux George, with sadomasochistic implications that were probably unsettling, having been conjured by a second-grader. The play ended with me atop a dirt mound in my yard, arms raised and reaching for the escape rope tossed by helicopter from the genuine Paul McCartney. Paul climbed down and risked his life, all the while singing "Here, There, and Everywhere." The whole thing satisfied my rescue fantasies and my need to be validated by a rock star while wearing a halter dress. I wrote a letter to a television station trying to get some interest, but my parents never mailed it.

By the time I found you I was still devoted to the Beatles but I was in high school and ready for something else. Rickie Lee Jones and The Smiths were a couple years away but your music was on time. It was a shove that made me want to fight back. My brother brought me your records one by one. We'd sit in his room and listen to each track with him jumping up and diving into air guitar or stopping to move the needle back so we could re-listen to a lyric. Sometimes he'd lend me one overnight so I could listen as I fell asleep, and when it ended I'd tiptoe over in my nightgown and start the whole record over with the volume lower. You were showing up on my porch when I listened to your records, driving me away in your banged-up car. This was better than my actual life and the metallic taste of rage on my tongue that I couldn't even locate or explain to anyone. You were a loner in a small town too, isolated and branded weird. I put on your records and imagined the two of us finding each other, both alienated and starving for affection. I snuck out my bedroom window to meet you in abandoned amusement parks and garages, I could feel your leather jacket against my cheek, and see the relief in your face when I showed up, someone who never accused you of sulking or being strange. For the whole length of your song we ran through alleys and whispered on pay phones. I nursed you after brawls in the parking lot, sneaking home your white T-shirt and scrubbing the blood out of it in secret, all the while defending you to my imaginary friends who worried about me for dating a monosyllabic hoodlum with a broken muffler.

No one wants to hear about the congenital melancholy that gnaws at the soul of a teenaged girl, and there was no one for me to tell. Skulking through life as a loser was oddly shaming though, and has continued to trail me through realities that flat out contradicted it. At sixteen I only wanted to be worth the level of beseeching I felt in the wail of your harmonica. It went inside me, that sound. It crept up and under my skirt and made my skin beg back. There had to be someone as lonely as me who needed to be kissed and infuriated in just the right way. *I know how to do all that* is what I thought.

It may be that everyone feels peripheral in high school. My one friend and I stuck together, but some days I would walk halfway to school in the morning only to turn around and go back. I started counting my credits in my head, one day realizing I could leave high school altogether in a few months if I took extra classes. "What about graduation? What about prom?" I heard a few ask. "Precisely," I thought to myself.

I packed up my records and went to live with my sister, who would instill me with some kind of confidence if it killed her, she would help find somewhere with others like me and stand quietly applauding when I took my first baby steps toward it. My first college dorm room had your album cover taped to the door. I was at arts school now, having finally said out loud that I wanted to be an actress, and I was in the right place. Nothing I could do on that campus was weird enough. Surrounded by every other rejected neighborhood freak, we were unleashed. Freedom didn't fit yet, but if I wasn't entirely authentic, I was making friends and jokes like I'd always known how. Boys were following me. I wore opera gloves to breakfast and held my unitard on with safety pins. My friend Ken and I did our one-man shows for each other (he in a straight-jacket, me in a coffin) and he'd sing Waits at the piano while I hung on him and wept. Joe M. called me "girl with no spine"; always draped over a boy like I had no bone or muscle to sit up on my own. We were happily unhinged, those of us who aspired to be Malkovich; to make theater that was incendiary and new. Led by my friend Peter, we started creating it in rehearsal spaces at night. When security banged on my door with a tornado warning, I gave them the finger. My legs were wrapped around the face of a green-eyed boy who also ignored that safety evacuation while you blasted from the turntable at a nearly unlistenable level. I couldn't get life loud enough.

The last time I saw you in concert I stood on the stage by the soundboard. The fact that you seem to know who I am is still confounding, but someone told you it was my birthday and you sang a song for me. I was about as close to detonation as I get.

Afterward I listened to you talk about the show. There is a level of purity in your approach that you could have left by the side of the road years ago. It doesn't come for free the way you do it and I get the feeling you couldn't live with yourself if you faked your way through. You said

We are the custodians of people's memories

You feel a responsibility to your audience when you play live. You said you can let it go the way of formula with everyone leaving reasonably sated, or invent it in the moment, which always comes with the risk of failure. It's your goal to go digging for it each time, letting it grow out and under the audience until they're part of its composition. I have to hold that up as a metaphor for everything, being prepared and then being brave enough to just be there. Just listen and follow, maybe jump. Everyone leans in, it brings them into your emotional vicinity, because, you said

Risk creates intimacy

That works everywhere, but onstage it's more common to opt for the easy way. It's a whole other gift when you relinquish being impressive in the moment to make it about the moment itself. Then the love you're getting back from the crowd is out of the picture. Without risk, it's just handing out a bunch of pie. Everyone is content but I'm not sure it endures or changes anyone. The clearest about this was maybe Bob Dylan. When asked how he could stand being booed and keep on playing, he said, "You got to realize you can kill someone with kindness, too."

Sometimes I still have to go back and sit on the swing set with you at midnight. Feel myself reflected in the broken but unbeatable gaze of another misfit toy. Your songs were so often about an elsewhere, a promised land where things would be okay, like the Three Sisters' insistent longing for Moscow. Amidst the slamming doors in your songs was a tenderness I was dying for. Listening to you sing about it, romance grew in me like a lotus in the mud, and you always held your car door open so nicely in my dreams. I could sigh just remembering it now. Always looking at me like I mattered, who cares if you were trapped inside vinyl. It got me through, dreaming of your backseat, and that was Moscow enough for me.

Dear Movement Teacher,

Any normal person can juggle. You made it clear that sure, certain people could not, but they were abnormally uncoordinated and would never be actors. I was on the fast track to failure being one of two people in the entire class who could not juggle. I could barely toss.

At breakfast the freshmen could be seen juggling biscuits. At lunch the lawn was littered with us juggling packs of Marlboro Lights while also smoking them, and at night some would exit the showers juggling sticks of deodorant. The hotshots would show off, but most were hoping just to pass the mandatory juggling exam held each week. I was privy to a lot of gruesome meltdowns on the hill that you didn't know about since teachers rarely wandered there. First-year drama students would buckle from the pressure. They'd throw their beanbags into the grass, swearing through clenched teeth. Everyone except me and one other girl,* though, could keep them in the air for at least a few seconds.

My friend P. was a proficient juggler, part of the group who could have been plucked off campus and shuttled away to Big Apple Circus. He would join the contingent on the lawn that could juggle while doing somersaults; he could have easily juggled while rebuilding the engine for someone's car. He was, in fact, in all the promo materials for the school, a photo of him looking gorgeous and juggling *while on a unicycle.* My friend M. was a competent juggler. M. didn't go to sleep chasing dreams of you lobbing swords at him until his head flew off. He only went to bed fearing I might have sex with his roommate while he had to pretend to be asleep. Sorry about that, M. I mean, guilty.

M. meditated a lot because his Aunt O. had sent him to a Transcendental Meditation teacher. I thought that was weird. He'd sit there on the freezing dorm room floor, eyes closed and drooling a little for twenty minutes twice a day. Years later I learned meditation and it changed me profoundly. I now sit there every day with eyes closed, but I hardly ever drool. I'm sorry that, okay, I also had some amount of sex with M.'s roommate while he was meditating ten feet away. It was his special time and that was creepy of me.

You as our teacher must have realized that we did things most college freshmen aren't expected to do. During voice class we jogged across campus in our "blacks," the spandex uniform

---

* (When I was a sophomore, my friend K. would be the non-juggler in his class. I knew we were soul mates when I saw his frozen, near-transcendent look of despair as he stared at those juggling balls on the ground, his suffering so acute that he almost glowed, like one of those laminated holy cards, a crown of beanbags on his head.)

we wore as first-year drama students, and as we jogged we held a piece of cork between our teeth to relax our jaw muscles. L., our voice teacher, sent us out the door, clapping her hands to establish a rhythm and urging us to "Flick those fetlocks! Flick! Flick them!" We trotted into other buildings where ballet dancers and opera singers would barely notice us jogging by while chanting SPA LA LA YA YA YA GA GA GA (with the corks it came out more PHA RA RA YUL YUL YUL CAW CAW CAW).

For the frontier exercise in acting class we sat with eyes closed, rocking side to side and waiting for the urge to roll or jump into the space and enter our "frontier." Landing in a difficult personal memory, we'd describe our feelings as the teacher walked us through the reexperiencing of it. Frontier involved weeping and shouting unintelligibly, whereas in speech class we articulated plosives and mastered "liquid u's" so that the word *duty* became more "dyutee" than "doody." In text class we sat on the floor in leg warmers taking copious notes while our chain-smoking professor broke down the import of the stress in "Our Town" being on "Town," and not "Our."

My other classes were not the same kind of struggle as yours. I did well in Marty's class with frontier and the "No Rose Without a Thorn"* exercise. In dance class I was not bad at the routine set to "Eye of the Tiger." We were stuffing in everything we could and

---

* We were in groups of four, and J. was the afterlife guide who took me away after I died while giving birth to E., who gained strength while searching for his father's love. T. played the father who died from anguish after my body was carried away, but we ended our silent improv with E. and I holding hands to symbolize our reunion after death. It went extremely well, better than our "Act of passion" silent improv, in which I played the statue symbolizing beauty that E. couldn't tolerate not fully possessing as his own, and subsequently destroyed.

generally having the time of our lives, yet still the elderly, the infirm, could juggle better than me. I sensed you suspecting that my special-needs juggling was emblematic of my inability to be "neutral." The drama faculty wanted us to find artistic "neutrality." If we didn't find it we could be drop-kicked all the way home, and my failure to find a neutral-suit made you throw up your hands. I tried but couldn't even fake it. It's a speed I don't offer on my gearshift. I was not issued the particular tool kit of middle. Gymnastics was also an issue. For those who couldn't swing a handspring by themselves, another student was poised at the spring-off point to "spot" us. When it was my turn the spotter would assume the posture, knowing deep down there would be nothing to spot. My handspring was basically me scurrying down the mat and reaching out with the beginnings of a cartwheel, then squatting and contracting into a ball as though I'd been hit with severe abdominal cramps. Then I'd pop up, arms raised and an impish expression on my face. I thought impish would suggest the spirit of those Russian girls in the Olympics with micro ponytails who never menstruate, but it only made me look spastic.

Gymnastics was a bust, but my low point was the day you were teaching the forward undulation walk. First you had us lie on the ground to relax our back muscles. I intentionally did not lie next to M. because I knew he'd try to make me laugh or he'd have a distracting erection, so I went over by V. and C. My class had a real camaraderie, even our wild parties or mini orgies* had

---

* Orgy was so mild. I think a teacher walked in on it and we actually sent a representative to apologize on behalf of the class. No wait, the teacher was driving the car. Van. It was the back of a minivan. There was another incident, at J. and C.'s house, well, never mind.

a ring of Swiss Family Robinson, and there was no sabotaging. As a result I didn't feel completely isolated when you marched over and snapped at me. "This isn't naptime! Wake up."

I wasn't tired or even spacing out. I was trying to let go of the blockage in my lower back, I triple swear, but the thing you could not have been expected to understand was that I have my entire life given people the wrong signals with my face, which was actually working overtime to find an expression that was neutral and someone who understood how to work in opposition, but I was not the sum of those faces. I was still the face that sometimes infuriated others against my will. (I know you thought my lizard was inappropriate during the animal exercise. I really don't recall trying to make my lizard overtly sexual, per se.) Regardless, in that moment I said nothing and stood up with the rest of the class. I was across from S. and we began undulating, but you were not happy and walked through the maze of black Danskins, waving your arms and telling us to just, please. Stop. You stood in front of us but facing the mirror. You shook your head, giving a Kabuki version of a shrug and then you said, "Don't you people understand about working in opposition!"

We did not.

I wonder if you still teach that? Where you catch an impulse and throw it to someone after undulating through your center? Forgive me but I feel like an impulse is not something you can catch. You can catch a ride to Mr. Waffle, you can catch herpes, but an impulse is supposed to spring *from you* and is mechanically antecedent to a reflex, because it can be squelched, whereas a reflex is automatic, isn't it? When impulses need curtailing, you have to learn "impulse control," so can you really see one coming from an outside source in sweatpants and, like, catch it? Wouldn't that be like catching someone's repression? Sorry, did you consider calling it "Catching a vibe," or even "Seize that wave"? I'm not certain it was useful. Maybe that's why we did it, though. To dive in and not ask why, maybe that was the point. I can say in retrospect that actually, to do a move so unsexy in front of your peers with or without a cork lodged in your jaw has to be useful. I'm wondering if I misunderstood the whole thing? It's possible that I exhibited some kind of rejection of it that showed on my face despite my protestations of being the most eager student ever. Wow. Okay, so maybe I was not entirely honest about me. Myself. For what it's worth I think I may get the value of it, however circuitous my arrival at this understanding may be. Yes. So it's safe to say I am late. In getting it.

On that day though, after admonishing the entire class you turned away from the mirror to face me, and said, only to my face, while pointing, also at my face

Why can't you get this Why can't you get anything

Cut to me pulling the midterm evaluation letter from my mailbox that had ARTS PROBATION stamped across it. The letter basically stated that I needed to fix myself or I would be gone.

I was ashamed and embarrassed. I hated that I would have to tell my father even though I knew he would take my side. I read the evaluation from you that explained why you had suggested that probation. You said that

She asks inappropriate questions that disrupt class

She appears spaced-out and bored

The lack of physical energy is alarming

Her use of sexuality is offensive

I was so mad. I felt like I was trying to be what you wanted and you were stuck in your categorical rejection of everything I was. Am.

I sulked but not so much that I would be caught caring what you thought of me. I went back to the dorm and sat holding the letter, reading and rereading the notice of my potential expulsion. My friend M. came in and asked what was up and I told him that you hated me. I said you were a turd and what you'd written on the evaluation was bogus. I showed him the letter and while still holding it and looking down at it without expression he asked me

What are you going to do about it

I said, "Do? What do you mean, 'do'? I've done everything I can. What he wrote isn't even an evaluation," and M. said

Yes it is. That's what he thinks of you, and he's the teacher so what are you going to do about it

I said, "But I feel like I was trying so hard already," and he said

It doesn't matter what you felt, what are you going to do

The last was a statement and not a question that slapped me so hard I couldn't look in his face. I sat staring at my feet. Whose side are you on, I asked, and he said yours, but you have to understand that he is the teacher. This is his evaluation of you. It's up to you to change his opinion.

The shift where I went from resenting him to my awakening that wow, this person is so correct was swift. I realized yes, this is a naked reality about myself that I have to address even if part of me is still cranky. It was a relief to see that maybe someone's dislike of me wasn't intractable, and to own up to the fact that a person who dislikes me isn't automatically to be dismissed, because: *sometimes I am deeply unlikable.*

Our very next class together, I went in with a different set of priorities and not wearing a backless unitard. I was actively defenseless as a choice.

When my father was at Officer Candidate School he was taken before the officers for a review. It was standard. The soldiers listened while every fellow before them was taken down for an infraction they'd committed and each man would respond. My dad started to notice sameness in tone with each testimony. Commanding officer would say, you did blah de blah, would you like to offer your explanation, and private whoever would say yes, sir, I realize what I did, but this is why and so on. After the eleventh or twelfth exchange, my dad said he realized that regardless of the excuse, they all came across as defensive and it weakened them. He felt inspired suddenly as he stepped before the Lt. Colonel, who asked if he'd like to offer an explanation for his misdeed. My dad said

No, sir, I would not

The already orderly room went silent. The Lt. Colonel looked up at my father and said, "What do you mean by that, Private?" My dad said

I offer no excuses, sir. I take responsibility and it won't happen again.

A few weeks into my new approach, I asked you a question after class. Truthfully I didn't have a question, I just wanted to connect. Anyway, your head tilted as you leaned in to listen. An adjustment of your eyebrows felt the tiniest bit artificial. You were arranging your face to come across as open and interested. I looked down, embarrassed that we were actually communicating; it felt sparked. I was meeting you, finally.

> **Me:** Sorry, could I ask you a quick question? *(I don't really have a question. Hi.)*
> **You:** Sure, how can I help? *(This is my interested face. I'm having trouble with the eyebrows.)*
> **Me:** So, when we freeze in the space after you clap your hands, are we supposed to be aware of anyone else? *(Honestly I'm so grateful that you said "How can I help" that I may cry.)*
> **You:** It's more about the freeze than what follows. Take a scan of yourself to see exactly where you are, which is—
> **Me:** Right! Right. Sorry. *(Shit! Shit. Sorry.)*
> **You:** For what?
> **Me:** I didn't mean to interrupt, sorry. *(PLEASE DON'T RE-HATE ME!)*

You: Well you're posing a good question, actually. *(I see that you are trying and I appreciate the effort.)*

Me: Oh, good. *(Your eyebrows are doing that welcoming thing again. Would it be awful if I hugged you?)*

You: But it speaks to a future exercise. For now stay focused on your own instrument. *(I'm glad we're connecting but I have another class now. Why are you hugging yourself?)*

Me: Great, I get it now. *(Your eyes are really sparkly. But like Santa. I'm not being inappropriate.)*

You: Good work today. *(Good work today.)*

Me: Thank you so much. *(I love you so much. Not to be gross, just thanks.)*

After that day your face softened. At the end of the semester I was doing an improvisation with H. and you lit up, burst out laughing.* I'd accomplished something bigger than comedy, and it proved that I needed to change. The person who deserves the credit for that laugh is unequivocally you. Letting someone you don't really like surprise you is evolved, and that would have been impossible if you didn't have the humility I wasn't giving you credit for. I was so caught up in your being wrong about me that I hadn't honestly taken you in. It's so transparent, how willing we are to dismiss the intelligence of someone who rejects us, as though that renders them incapable of sound judgment.

The last time I saw you, we were backstage after a play I was

---

* We were minions who earned a wage by living under the ball gowns of rich women and holding up the fabric of their skirts so they wouldn't trip while they danced.

doing. You were so generous and that made me feel like a million bucks. It would have been so sad if I'd spent all those years and never reintroduced myself; I would have missed out on all of your special wisdom, not to mention the thrill of the view up there on the high road.

Thank you for being open to another more workable draft of me. It affected me profoundly. I still can't juggle. I mean to say that I can't juggle in your way, as certain metaphorical methods I am actually acing on a daily basis, but biscuits or beanbags would be a negative. I confess that during the writing of this piece I snuck into my son's room and took the juggling sacks off of his shelf. I gave it a shot. I thought you might like to hear that it wasn't as bad as I thought at first, but then very swiftly it was maybe even worse than I thought. It doesn't seem to be in the cards. You'd be happy to know that I'm actually working on a certain kind of neutrality. I know, shocking, but I see the value in it now.

Dear Blue,

Did you sew it? I'm just trying to imagine where you got it. There was no such thing as Amazon yet and I'd never seen one, except on Tarzan.

Your loincloth. Did you use fabric from an old couch? You didn't have a couch. Maybe you liberated a square of fabric from your tepee or stitched together some burlap bags that once held hydroponic fertilizer.

You wore that cloth on your loins every day so maybe there was even a spare? You were a fruitarian, eating nothing but fruit and nuts (though apparently beer was also a fruit?); a van illegally parked on the beach (not beside it, on it) was your home; and you needed no shirt, shoes, nothing. You and your friend Gary drove to the border at dawn to get avocados and figs for the co-op where I worked also and then you went to the beach if you had no one to rolf. You were a rolfer, too, massaging those lucky people while wearing nothing or your loincloth. Okay, maybe a piece of jewelry was also on your body. A conch-shell necklace, but that was it. You and Gary both had gorgeous, ocean-soaked hair that was longer than mine. Gary had a mane of chestnut that might have made him rich if he'd opened a Seven Stations of the Cross theme park, but your hair was its own Disneyland. It glowed in the dark from salt water and sun. That hair gave you the vibe of being both switched on and overcooked at the same time. You were the only men I've ever seen who could wear your hair in a bun with a flower and not seem sissy. You had soul patches and tans, period. Diving in the surf might happen five times a day, and how could you lie down at the tide and feel sand rushing everywhere if you were wearing clothes? When you took me to that nude beach up the coast, taking off your loincloth seemed brazen. A dog could walk away with your entire wardrobe in its mouth. Ripping it off was a breeze though, and you threw yourself in the water leaving me in awe of how little there was between you and the world. It took hardly anything to be not just happy, but filled with a kind of alien joy.

You took anyone's idea of modern life and set it on fire decades before anyone dreamed up Burning Man. You didn't need to rent an RV with Wi-Fi and stock up at Whole Foods to drive somewhere and let the madman into your third eye. You'd found it and let it all in and out again and had it going on. Even your name, which you said had become you after you'd dropped acid and were sitting on a massive rock by the cliffs. When you opened your eyes, everything including you was blue. Everything except your loincloth, which, for the summer I knew you, was a light brown man wrap that made you and Gary look like Malibu Jesus dolls and kept you from being arrested for indecent exposure by more or less covering your genitalia. You and Gary would come into the co-op first thing

in the morning with Minnie Riperton pouring out of your van. The
two of you would pelt me with flowers while I sat in the back of the
stockroom bagging and weighing organic nuts, rennet-free cheese,
and bizarre dried sea vegetables. Back then only the hard-core who
came to our store even knew about dried kelp. In the eighties only
true hippies bought spirulina in a bag and snorted it, or however
they took it once I'd bagged and labeled it probably incorrectly,
and priced it, most definitely incorrectly. Some days, joining me
at the scale was a sweet and sullen transgender boy named Luxe
who wasn't much better than I was. We got in trouble for throwing a block of Gouda up at the ceiling fan to see if it would come
down in chunks, so they separated us. They had one of us bag while
the other stocked dairy, which meant standing in the refrigerator
and replenishing all the yogurt and kefir and freezing our asses
off. I found the scale confusing and was never good at math, so I'd
spend hours getting yelled at by that girl named Jacque who was
a higher-up. I heard you used to date her, which I had a hard time
picturing. Jacque dressed in those macramé tops that she made and
tie-dyed, and she sewed her own maxi pads with inspiring words
inked on in beet juice to make her connect to her yoni. I don't know
if you were into this also but Jacque drank her pee, which (once she
blew in my face lightly then asked me, hey does my breath smell like
urine?) was brave in a way, but she was hard to admire because she
admonished me daily for being inept. She said my mistakes made
her feel confused and out of touch. Freshly punished, I'd go back to
my station and try to get the plankton or ground matcha out from
under my fingernails, wishing I didn't have to work two jobs, or
that one of them didn't have to be this one which sometimes paid
me in avocados. She clearly still had a thing for you because she

hated me not only for my mistakes but also for your chilling with me while I unwittingly butchered all the price tags. You came over one day when she'd been particularly harsh and said

Hey, come on, she can't fire you. If you were fired all the men who work here would protest

At first I didn't know how to talk to you because you were so calm and genuine. Your voice was deep and slow. When I talked you would sometimes just stare at my mouth. After I'd been there a while you said

When I met you I thought, God, this girl must spend hours in front of the mirror watching her mouth

To make enough money to live, I took a bus away from beach life and worked at a coffee shop. The first morning that I was entrusted with opening the shop, I locked all the customers out on the street. I'd somehow barricaded myself inside the shop and couldn't open the door. The undercaffeinated patrons were outside knocking on the glass while I kept trying the key and combination over and over. I put my face in my hands when the customers began to get twitchy. "I'm so sorry," I mouthed to them through the glass, "I'm open to suggestions from any of you?" One woman cupped her hands around her mouth and pressed them on the glass, shouting "SECOND LOCK. THERE IS A SECOND LATCH. LOOK UP," but after turning it several times with no clicking sound I told them through tears to please just go away. To my horror the manager showed up and shouted commands at me until the door finally opened and then she banished me behind the counter to grind beans, which I enjoyed because the sound of the grinder disallowed conversation. While my beans were grinding that morning I leaned on the machine and felt the vibrations through my arm like a little massage. Staring into the parking lot, I squinted when I saw a familiar broken-down van barreling around with windows open and loud music leaking out. I started to pace, not knowing where to hide as the van pulled into a spot and the doors flew open. A cloud of smoke rolled forth followed by you and Gary walking toward my fancy coffee shop in your loincloths. You had no shoes on and even though none of us wore shoes at the health food store (earth to health department) I was wearing shoes then and I had on a sensible sundress. Seeing you outside the context of the health food store I was struck by the fact that you were essentially nude. I could not have you in the coffee shop where I was barely still working. I didn't want to hurt your feelings or make you not like me but I was pretty sure that my boss would not want you near the pastry counter with your pubes visible and flying free. I froze. I couldn't move for a moment because there was and still is something I was not and remain not skilled at voicing and that is the phrase NOW IS NOT THE TIME CAN WE DO THIS LATER. PLEASE.

I hid. From you and Gary. Under the bean bins, or actually in front of them because a customer was in the bathroom and there was nowhere else to go. This is where I become confused. The bizarre thing is that now, decades later, despite remembering that day and that whole summer distinctly, I don't remember what happened next. I can recall the manager seeing me and I remember gesturing wildly to her that two humans were walking in who shouldn't, but I don't know what happened after that. Did I block out that part because I regret being such a coward? It feels shameful that I hid from you two, who were so sweet and didn't even drink coffee. I remember thinking I would be in trouble with the manager if two nude men with better hair than her came into her shop. I have a hazy memory of speaking to you at the counter, but that could be a rendition I created where I acted like a rational person who stood up and said hey. What did I do, would you remember?

I would run into you as I walked the neighborhood with that enormous black dog named Bear, a Chow who was mysteriously waiting for me every time I left my house. Bear would sit outside the Laundromat when I went in with my friend Natalie on Friday nights. Natalie and I would combine all our wash to save money and we'd dance on top of the machines with some mild flashing of body parts to passersby if we'd drunk a few beers. Bear would stand outside and bark at men who saw us through the windows and tried to enter with no laundry. He'd sit there and when I left, he left. Natalie said he belonged to a family on the block and wasn't neglected, but maybe he needed someone to protect. One night Luxe and I were walking to the beach with Bear and I heard a honk. It was you and Gary smoking a joint and waving for us to get in. Bear growled and bared his teeth and Luxe said

No, please, those guys freak me out with their Jungle Book cock hankies

I said we were on the way to see Luxe's mom and you drove off singing and blowing me a kiss. When I saw you in the store the next day I was pricing walnuts and only half listening to Marshall, the guy who worked in the book section. Marshall was nice and highly intelligent. He could recite half-hour polemics about Irish politics that he thought I was deeply interested in because I listened to U2. He'd bring me graphic photos of children disfigured by plastic bullets and literature about Northern Ireland that I pretended to read. You stood behind him eating a fig. I was scooping my walnuts when Marshall abruptly leaned in and said something I never saw coming on the heels of him having just handed me a picture of a little girl whose nose was blown off

So, ma chere, would you like to come over and spend the night on Friday?

Now:

A. He was not French. He was from Humboldt County.
B. He'd never even flirted with me unless you count him giving me an underground "death index" listing all the people killed by plastic bullets. Admittedly, he said I could keep it and it was his only copy.
C. I'd never flirted with him. Maybe he took my gazing into his eyes bored as my gazing into his eyes wanting him?
D. There was the chance that he wanted quality time to go more in-depth about politics?

"D" was blown when I said, "Okay, sure," and he did a tiny thumbs-up and smiled.

I said okay. Not just okay, but "okay, sure," a double affirmative. We'd gone from "Good morning. I have more detail to share

re suffering in the North of Ireland" to "I will thrust a chubby inside of you Friday night. Let me know if you are allergic to cats."
Why didn't I ask, hey, do you mean so we can listen to *Under a
Blood Red Sky* and order Burger King? Or are you thinking the
other kind of special sauce? And how unfair of me to say yes when
no way was I going to his leprechaun cottage to eat boiled pota-
toes and listen to bootlegs of Crass.

So Marshall sauntered off, certain I was coming over to suck
his rubber bullet, and why wouldn't he? I'd said okay, sure.

I didn't look up when you slid over to my scale and said

Hey sunshine

You'd heard the whole thing. You asked if I was going to spend
the night with Marshall and I said, no, looking over at that Nordic
Percussionist sitting in the office. He was pretending to work on
the books while reading the Tao Te Ching. You said you're not
seeing that guy, are you, rolling your eyes, and I said kind of, and
you said are you or aren't you? I said maybe. You said why didn't
you just say no thanks to Marshall. I said I don't know how to
say no, I only know how to yell it. I didn't want to hurt his feelings. You said, what does he care, just say no and move on, and
I was like, yeah, let me work on communicating like a grown-up.
You smiled at me, leaning on my table and not speaking. I smiled
back, my scooper still stuck in a bag of health powder. We were
interrupted by Saturn Johnnie, the LSD casualty who worked in
produce. He popped over and said, "Blue, hi, I want a second with
her, or really, just stay, that's also fine, I wanted to mention that
it's retrograde Mercury time and some of us will be dropping acid

in my yard tonight and gentle body painting is involved? If you'd care to join?"

I stared at him. No one moved. I started to say "Maybe I will come later," but I got out "May——" and Blue put his hand over mine, and said

Sorry, man, she's hanging with me tonight, we've planned it since forever.

Saturn Johnnie said, "Oh, sure. Well come together if you want to share. It's BYOB." Blue said some other time and Johnnie left and I said, you see, I am not good with no.

Blue said

Don't get introverted. The sun is shining. You are your usual outer-planetary self. We're all just trying to laugh and get home safe

You were all right with yourself and knew how to say no. There was no one for you to impress and no one for you to offend. You were right there and I was afraid of how real you were, which made me question my own level of authenticity. I'd take off my clothes on the beach or spill my guts to a girl I'd never met on the bus, thinking I was uncensored and open, but I wasn't always real if I wanted someone to like me. I gravitated to those who withheld or told me who they thought I was. What would have happened if I'd shown up at your van to hang out? If it weren't for my friend Natalie digging you I might have but I'm sure your silence would have scared me. There was no game to play. The games wore me out in the end but back then I was weak for anyone with an excess of charisma. I kept saying I wanted sweetness and someone truthful but I was fussy about the form that sweetness might take. I wonder where you are out there. I hope your goodness is intact and you still feel blue all over. Really I want to say I'm sorry for hiding from you behind the coffee bins and whatever else I put in front of me, attempting to keep genuine kindness away.

Dear Abraham,

You took me in when I scratched at your door, needing someone with your skill set.

I had come to your office and just sat down, about all I could really manage. You'd been talking for an hour and I slouched there full of echoes. My eyes were dark and unreadable in that younger face. I had to grow into myself and lose the air of someone who was recently electrocuted but didn't seem to mind it. I do remember that I couldn't speak when you said,

"I don't want to alarm you but according to the bank, you don't have any available funds. You have no apparent savings. To live on, et cetera. At this time."

I gathered my hair into one hand and made a sound like a hose being turned on.

"Okay, so," you said. You seemed unsure if I was devastated or hypoglycemic. "Shall I explain this to you? Do you understand how this happened?"

"No. But I mean, yeah, if you want to try? I mean, I'm not very . . ." I crossed my eyes and sat back. I stared at your paper clips wishing I could shift them with my mind. I was embarrassed to be broke and to not know that I was broke.

Your intercom rang.

"Sorry, one second, all right? I need to answer this," you said, picking up the phone and pushing a button. I did not move, and you said again, "Give me one second," and waved at me to see if I was breathing, a gesture I was so used to that I no longer even responded to it.

"You. Would you like anything to eat?"

"No. Or wait. Yeah, no," I said.

"Could I ask you something?" you asked, putting the phone down and hanging up on whomever.

"Oh, sure," I said.

"How did your shirt get ripped like that? Were you attacked? I mean, I'm asking." Your hands were out on either side, bent at the waist in a shrugging, "what can I say" posture. Like a penguin trying to fly with half-assed effort. The gesture seemed to cover a lot of common communications for you, such as: "Well, there you go," and "Nobody asked you, okay?" and "If you already put the mustard on it, I'll live."

"I bought it that way," I said. But was I supposed to show you a receipt? I realized that I for sure did not have one, because now that I thought about it the shirt wasn't mine.

"Oh, wait," I said. "It's actually my friend Olivia's? But, yes. She bought it like this. Unless, I mean, she stole it?" I laughed, and suddenly wished I hadn't said that.

"What, stole? From whom, stole? She's what, a criminal?"
You were almost shouting but for some reason I didn't panic.

"No, no. I mean, maybe she did that once, I don't know. She's
a stripper so she always has a lot of ones? Sometimes she's, like,
embarrassed to pay with one-dollar bills because it makes her
seem like a stripper." I wanted him to know Olivia was essentially
a good girl. Who only rarely stole from Fiorucci.

"We have to get you some new friends." You said, "Seriously,
that's no good."

"I know, but she is mostly great. I don't ever, I mean, steal,"
I said.

You did the arm gesture. I was trying to think of something
to say about how I could stop being broke. I sighed again, louder
than what is actually polite and you looked like you felt badly for
me, which made me embarrassed and a little drowsy. I had to take
three subways and walk eight blocks to get home from there because I had to pick up something in Midtown and this meeting was
still going on and now there was this whole poverty thing.

"You are, what, pardon me, but what are you, twenty-three?
Twenty?" You were speaking softly, like maybe the room was
bugged and my age was top secret.

"I guess," I said.

There was another ample chunk of no talk.

You decided to be blunt, just say the thing.

"So you are looking for a new accountant, or what?"

You asked this question too loudly and at the first two words,
which broke the silence, I jumped a little. I wished for the mil-
lionth time that I'd been born with a remote control. I tried to

make my face seem intent but reasonable. "I guess I didn't know, you know. My situation . . ." I could feel my voice trailing off but could not come up with a point so I kept on, "And yeah," I said, pointing to the papers on your desk that I had brought in a Chinese food take-out bag, "I don't understand those statements and I thought I had money? Because, like, they said I had some, or actually, they never specifically indicated that I didn't? I asked them if I could buy the pool table, I called them from the pool table . . . place, and they said knock yourself out, so it's not like I was trying to spend it all but . . . I guess I sometimes wanted to pay? For stuff? Because I was living with someone who had money and I didn't want him to always pay, because. I didn't."

This is the most I'd said since I sat down and maybe the biggest speech of my week. I watched you take it in. I knew that I was unclear and you probably didn't want to ask me to clarify, which is why you appeared torn, or maybe you were tired, but something about me was making you edgy. You looked like you had to stop yourself from shouting at me but part of me just wanted you to shout.

"Well, what would you do with a pool table? Are you Irish?"
You laughed. I shrugged.

"My boyfriend. For Christmas. I mean, whatever." I felt the urge to cry so I distracted myself by digging around in my bag until I came up with a single piece of bubble gum. "He liked it." I rolled my eyes to keep from looking like a female.

"Well it seems," you said softly, "it seems that you could not afford that pool table"—I nodded as you spoke so you'd know that I understood—"and I guess there is no way to return it? I mean, for a refund?"

I shook my head no.

You decided to get back to the point.

"So Johnnie tells me that you are looking for a new accountant?" You were hoping this would begin to wrap things up so I would leave. "You are in need of financial advisers."

I looked up from the floor and smiled. You made a wheezing noise. I nodded yes.

Picking up a box of Kleenex and waving it around a little you said, "Well okay, then," and put the box back down.

No one said anything again. Your intercom buzzed but you didn't answer it.

"Hey," I said, standing up and discovering I was maybe six inches taller than you, "is it all right, I mean, are you okay if I lie down? I am so, I mean, you know." I picked up my purse and put my leather jacket on, still talking. You realized I was the sort of person who you could just tune out sometimes and I probably wouldn't care, and this made you like me. You were not listening now but I was still talking and walking toward your sofa. You wondered if your soup had arrived and questioned the last-minute change from chopped salad. When fresh, the chopped salad was very satisfying. For whatever reason, you decided that you chose wisely and that it would behoove you to be pleased with the soup. You have found that making these decisions in advance and sticking to them could sometimes circumvent disappointment. You glanced at your watch and tuned back in to me, but my voice was now unintelligible because I had my back to you, already curled into a black and yellow comma on your couch.

You walked to the door and opened it. This might not look so good, you thought, with me on the sofa. You went back and sat.

Suddenly you heard me whisper, "Can I smoke in here?" You leaned in and saw that my eyes were closed and I was breathing evenly. I seemed strangely even more familiar to you in sleep.

You took off your glasses and put them back on to get a better picture. Were those army shoes? With diaper pins? And there was some kind of graffiti on the back of the leather jacket. "Panther Elixer," it said, with symbols in orange. The dark red tights over black tights, with holes in them; were they on purpose? Were they purchased like that or were they normal and ripped later by hand? You tried to imagine buying a suit at Bloomingdale's and then taking it home and ripping it. Shredding it on purpose. You wondered: Do you laugh when you do it, the ripping? Was it a fun thing, done in groups? Or do you do it from anxiety, like a fetish? You have always wondered these things when you saw kids on the subway, looking like they'd gone at their clothing with a lawn mower.

"What, wait, is she sleeping?" asked Sandra as she entered with your soup. "That's the girl who came just now? You put her to sleep that fast?"

"Get out, already, how do I know? She says she's tired, what am I supposed to say?" You opened your Orangina. "You didn't get a straw."

"It's in the thing." Sandra fished it out and handed it to you. "She seemed nice, right?"

"How do I know? She's asleep. I'll ask her when she wakes up. If she is nice. All I know is she's broke." You inhaled the steam from the matzo ball and it had a calming effect. Sandra left, shaking her head.

Just then my hand flopped out and with a soft click a piece of bubble gum fell to the ground.

"What am I supposed to do with this?" You asked this of no one and I did not stir. You considered calling the rabbi for counsel.

In ten years you will consider walking to synagogue to ask the rabbi for counsel when you hear that I am at an ATM with a nonfunctioning debit card, since it is Shabbat and you cannot call me and you will wait until one minute past Shabbat to call me to help fix it. In twenty years, you'll go to your office on your day off to look for a copy of my son's passport because they do not allow him to board the plane since it has expired, and two days later after getting my son's passport replaced you'll wait in line with me while I am sobbing at Passport Express when I lose my own passport, only to take me the following day, again sobbing, to a passport expeditor when my new replacement passport goes missing two hours after I receive it. You will stand in line with me to wait to take my passport picture and you will hit me on the head with your hat when I ask you if my hair looks stupid.

In twenty-five years I will meet you near the synagogue to give a speech in your honor, and I will cry in front of the rabbi and all the people eating their kosher chicken when I say that you've treated me like a daughter and taken me from someone who couldn't afford a taxi to being someone who has her own driver. I will tell the story of how I fell asleep on your couch the day I met you and everyone will laugh.

For now you get on with it. So what there is a girl asleep on the couch over there. So what.

You go back to work and pause for a saltine. There is a little triumph in pulling one completely intact from its package. Uncracked. Why someone would defile a perfect saltine with soup, with wet, making it soggy and flaccid, is beyond you. You reach for another, which emerges also perfectly.

You buzz Sandra on the intercom.

"Is she still asleep?" Sandra asks.

"Mind your beeswax," you say, brushing the saltine dust on the floor. "Get me a Dustbuster. And an ashtray."

You stare at the crumbs so you won't lose them. You will know where they are when she arrives with the Dustbuster. You wait there like that.

Dear Popeye,

You said you would love me until you were ashes.

You bolted from work that morning and took a cab sixty blocks for a fuck-our-lights-out festival, you busted in and took me from dreams by throwing your backpack on my floor and then throwing down the pussy gauntlet; I roused and rallied and smiled and you tossed me across the bed—you could have had me fine in the direction I was facing, but it was a morning that needed a body happily pitched across a duvet with a guttural mm hmm, a morning that begged for bodice ripping and hair-pulling and whispering and taking off and taking me away, and just then—when I was waking the homeless on the streets with my OH GODS, you slammed into neutral at the end of the *in* part of the next *in* and *out*, you pulled fully out of me and backed off the bed like I was a parking space you were deciding against after several attempts to nail; you stood up so obscenely perfectly stiff and lumbering slightly, no false grace or attempt to indicate to me that: Hey! Woman with your legs as open as the E-ZPass track, I am coming back! No, "hang on one second," no halftime announcements, nothing, and so I was not sure if I should applaud, feel indignant, or just say screw that and start scrapbooking or what; so I stayed splayed and thrown and eventually started to think about maybe going to the gym, or the bodega, maybe today was the day I would learn how to use a Waterpik; at which point I heard, what, you opening my fridge? Looking for something in a drawer? Imodium? *Brian's Song?* On VHS? But then I heard a pop and a fizz and you appeared again, Renaissance Fair stud, with your cock in one hand, not because it needed reminders but because you wanted it in that hand while the other hand gripped a bottle of Coke Classic, the old-school kind, which—doesn't it? Taste so much better like that? Held in glass so you can see it as clearly as yesterday; you were singing "Harmony," I think, by Elton John, or no, "Melissa" by the Allman Brothers, and as you approached the bed you smiled and waved at me like I was across the street and you knew me from church or something, but I was right there and you were right there too and then even more there, inside me, and you had a grip on the headboard pulling yourself in, another hand holding your Coke so it wouldn't spill because you hadn't taken a sip yet, but you did, then, you stopped mid *in* or *out* or who remembers, took a long pull on the bottle while your free fingers started at my hair and moved down my front to my softest, where you were held so completely and you came at me both hard and soft and just when that stopped being strange, your having a bottle at your mouth, you pulled it away from your mouth, my eyes opening then as your hand found my cheek, not gently but not rough, either, and your mouth it was still full but you didn't swallow, you leaned in with lips near to spilling over and I parted my lips because I knew to and I like to obey when I can decode the command and you put your two lips on my two and opened your mouth, the Coke still cold and pepper sweet as you so slowly, like a faucet just left on by accident, you on purpose let it in my mouth and said

I thought you might be thirsty, baby

and I said oooooooooooohhhhhhhhhhh, oh yeah.

and it was loud, the next part, very loud, and we took it very seriously, and then it was quiet and there was some near-sleep and when I curled into the great wall of you, which was still not ordinary, still fragrant with your new exotic familiarity, I said a bold thing, which a girl who doesn't speak much can sometimes pull off, but I wasn't pulling this time, I wanted to say it, I said, "I feel full. I feel, if we were forever poor, and had to live with so little, you know, really poor, and this was the best thing we got, I would be all right with that," and you said

but we're all poor people. this is the best we get

Today I heard your voice. Years after losing each other, you've managed to hold to loving me still, in the way you can when you know you both tried.

I remember when you went off to trek the Pyrenees, you brought me flowers you picked from the top of a mountain there, carried them back in a tiny woven basket that I saved to this day, even though the flowers are dust. I wrote about us while you were away in a notebook that eventually saw the end of us, but the last I wrote about that time was in ink; it was a hurried, angry scrawl reading: Time, that cold bastard, with its nearlys and untils. I think, what a shame. Time should weep for having spent me without you.

Dear Man Out of Time,

That was quick, what we had.

I saw you on the couch at the party I didn't want to attend. Your legs were crossed in elegant trousers that exposed a length of what had to be a cashmere sock. "That's a gentleman," I thought, and I watched the way you held a glass and a conversation until I realized I wasn't looking at anything or anyone else.

I came out of the corner to sit beside you. Fairly quickly something sparked that was past flirting; and the scent of you was enough to keep me there. It was a mix of rituals from a perfectly groomed man who had one foot in another era: pressed shirts, oiled loafers and aftershave, but an old-fashioned, distinctly masculine smell. I wondered if you went to the races and wore suspenders on Sunday. I wanted to put my head on your shoulder and make a wrinkle there.

"Don't stop talking to me, ever," I thought. "You are the most interesting man on Earth." I kept asking you more and more questions and you turned your whole body to face me. We were both animated and nearly ignoring everyone else, but someone walked by smoking, you clearly knew him and pointed accusingly, laughed and said

When are you going to put those out?

I said something flip. I can't remember what. It was some reference to vices being our true comrades. The people sitting on either side of you were quiet. One smiled uncomfortably. You pointed to your head, which was bald, and I realized then, my mouth dissolving into a silent "Oh," that you hadn't shaved your head as a style choice for a dapper man losing his hair.

Well, it's . . . I have cancer, you see. It's unfortunate.

You tossed it off. A gracious dance move by a partner who didn't want anyone to see that their partner had tripped. You went back to talking about your girlfriend who I'd been asking about, as you had my boyfriend. We were both articulating, by extolling the virtues of our partners, that we were committed to our mates. Once that was laid out we were free to keep talking without worrying the other was receiving any incorrect signals. We were both so amped up by our interaction that it had to be established so we could get on with it. There was such freedom talking to you and no obligatory small talk. Your smile felt so alive with affection but there was a fixed quality to your face, as though you were memorizing me. You seemed poised to catch my phrases and pocket them with their accompanying silences. I felt like I was the Super

Bowl, you were that engaged, but with the permission to say, "Wait, what did you mean?" when I didn't get something. There was no squirming when the quiet went on too long.

Scientists can't agree where speech evolved from so no one can arrive at what makes a particular communication successful. This is something I would never ever want to know the secret to any more than I would want to know on which day I will die; but it's a subject I could pull apart for hours without getting bored. I love attempting to describe a thing, but I might love even better the fact that the more words you have available to encode with when you attempt denotation, the farther away you can sail into ambiguity. I could go on about you forever and that might only make you less clear to someone discovering you through my words. We might have had another twenty years to reveal ourselves to each other and not come away as sure of each other as we did.

Part of why we can't explain the origin of language is our reaction to perceived truth. If words were entirely reliable they would have evolved as the most efficient means of communication, but they haven't, because humans lie. An ape makes a sound or gesture to another ape signaling that it wants a banana. It gets the banana or not, but the communication is clear. An ape would never say, in ape-speak, "Your socks say a lot about you and I am intrigued. Would you mind handing me that banana?" Despite the fact that animals do "deceive" one another, they are resistant to deceit when they sense it. An ape would simply ignore a communication that was too convoluted, which I think would be a big fat relief. Humans are saddled with so many terrific ways of overcomplicating what we want. "I will give you five dollars for that banana," or "How come Jolene gets a banana and I don't?" Or even "I think we can both agree that after what happened last night, you owe me a fucking banana." All of this takes us further away from what is ultimately: Banana. Give it. We have all these fancy ways to say things, so why do we end up walking away from a simple interaction wondering, "What did they mean by that?" I don't know what made me want to sit there next to you or why talking to you felt so energizing. Is it how you were stringing words together or what was behind those words or both? I didn't need to interpret you, I wanted to take your hand and kept touching your arm. I nearly grasped it at one point, but the way you would with a brother or long-lost friend. It was everything minus the one thing that usually ruins it all in the end. I don't know what you call the sum total of that.

I left that night with your number and an appreciable craving to see you again. Weeks went by before we could make a date that we could both finally keep and I headed uptown that afternoon to see you for our unique nondate, fantasizing about what it would be like to see you once a week.

Your girlfriend answered the door, lovely and welcoming. She said you were in the bedroom not feeling well and I tried to convey that I was sorry. I wasn't expecting you to be unwell and worried that I should just slip away, but then you came out to greet me. You looked pale and a bit thinner but still dashing. I suggested that I should go and let you rest, directing my question to your girlfriend out of respect, but you wanted to have lunch. "I've been looking so forward to this. I'm not missing it," you said, and your girlfriend nodded her agreement and patted me on the shoulder as we left.

We walked to a place very near you and picked a table outside. I saw that you were moving much more slowly than you had a couple of weeks before. We ordered sparkling water and Italian food and it didn't take much time to connect. Our conversation was slower but the comfort was still there and your indescribable smile that made me have to restrain my impulse to take your face in my hands and kiss you, but without tongues and apologies and pulses flaring. I wanted to curl up next to you but not end up on top of you. It was clear and it came with boundaries that I would never have to draw. I just liked you so much.

As we left the restaurant you offered me your arm and I looked at you standing half in and half out of that bistro. The city instantly seemed to exist only to blend with the portrait of you there, poised to go for a walk with me. It was maybe like seeing Fellini in Rome. All of Manhattan was either moving past or revolving around you, creating the effect of the city explaining itself by way of a man representing it. The cafes and boutiques, all the well-dressed women going by became saturated with color when they moved into your frame and you completed their picture. The Guggenheim Museum, a group of little boys in school uniforms—all of it seemed constructed to exist as the atavistic backdrop that told your story.

I took your arm and it was clear you needed support. I found the place between us where I could balance and bring myself to you securely. The gesture found me for the first time trying to think of the right thing to say.

You spoke first. We were such a nice surprise, you said, and a reminder that things could still keep popping up. We had something unique you wanted to keep for your own, and you leaned over when you said, "This is for me, I need this." You looked down at me and said, oh, this is sweet and so good for me, but

this may be the world's shortest friendship

We spoke again once or twice, I think. I came home from a trip a month or so later and a card was waiting from your girlfriend. She told me I'd mattered to you and given you a kind of boost. I held the card to my face, covering my eyes, and saw us walking down the street. I remembered how everything fell into place on all sides of you like someone was off somewhere pushing buttons and calling cues.

Thank you for giving me your arm and those four hours that I now understand you did not have an endless supply of.

It was short but I loved our little trip. We fell in love, but the way you love a view that comes along once or twice in life. You don't want to leave it because it feels like, yes of course, this is the perfect spot. Those moments always come with a little shock and I love that sensation, when you think, this is too good, I'll catch up with everyone else later. You just have to take in the truth of that expanse a few more seconds before it changes and becomes something else entirely, or before you do.

Dear Father Bob,

I believed in you, who knew God and still liked him.

One Sunday when I was maybe eight, I leaned out of my pew as you were passing after the service. I reached up and pulled at your robe.

"Father Bob?" I whispered. You bent down to hear me over the organ. "Is there anyone in Hell?" I asked, knowing you would know. You knew enough to give my brothers and my sister and me Cheetos when we came to your house to play Ouija board. You could answer this.

Putting your hand on my shoulder, you paused. Your eyes moved back and forth like you were reading invisible text while I stayed fixed on you, awaiting the truth. You started to speak and then stopped.

"Now? You mean is anyone there now?" you asked. I nodded a solemn yes and you scanned my face again, considering, and said, "No."

"Okay," I said.

You patted me on the back as if to say, *good for you for question-ing what you think you're supposed to believe*, as though the idea of eternal damnation was absolutely something to be revisited, years after having been ordained. As though the afterlife was worth ex-amining upon being challenged by a third-grader. I realized that *it was your opinion, in that moment.* Faith to you was more clay than mortar, and if you could interpret the gospel, so could I. So should anyone. If God wasn't mad at you for drinking wine and chain-smoking and being a homosexual, he might forgive me for stealing a kitten and trying to hide it under a blanket in the back of our station wagon. Certainly that God was preferable to others who wouldn't let you in Heaven if you said bad words or drank Mountain Dew. If all your answers weren't in the Bible then mine didn't have to be, and potentially the point was to try to be honest and sweet like you, and not panic if you yelled or had too much spaghetti. You didn't worry that the Parker kids were going to burn in a smelly inferno just because they were trying to conjure dead spirits courtesy of Hasbro.

All us kids have stories about you. My oldest brother remem-bers you driving him in your own car all the way to Bisbee so he could deliver his declaration against the Vietnam War to the draft board. They took one look at him, skinny and asthmatic and already spouting his political diatribe to anyone who would lis-ten, and went to another section to find his name. They promptly informed him that he was F-4 status, a medical reject. He nearly burst into tears, having been robbed of the chance to articulate his opposition to the war by way of a narrative speech with footnotes. He paced the hall outside the draft board with you following him and listening to him go all over the map. What on earth should he do now, when he had not gotten what he did not want?

Finally he arrived at an idea, announcing that he had the answer: he would combine law and the teachings of God. "I will go to school and get my degree in canon law!" he said, excitedly, looking to you for validation. When he asked if you'd help steer him to this chosen path, you took a long drag on your cigarette and said

Of course I will. You realize, though, that canon law is about as useful as tits on a butterfly

"I know someone who can answer that better than me," I said to my children. It was thirty years after my question to you in church that day and my own kids had one now. They bounced on the bed while I dialed you at home.

"Guys, settle," I said, "this man is a big deal to Mommy and I'm putting him on speaker."

"Is he nice?" asked my son.

"Father Bob?" I heard coughing after a faint "hello." It was your voice. I hadn't heard you in years but the sound of you was a time machine. I asked how your partner was, and you said great and he was right there in fact. I said to give him my best and incidentally, would you mind answering my kid's question about what went down when Jesus died and you said sure thing. I nudged my son, who was trying to pry a rubber chicken out of my daughter's hands. He put his face up next to the phone and said hello.

"Hello to you," you said.

"Well," said my son, "why did he come out of that cave? That had the big rock in front."

"There was a rock?" asked my daughter. My son punched her, whispered be quiet and she punched him back, said she didn't have to. I'm killing you both, I whispered, just stop it now and then I said full voice to you,

"They were confused about how he came out."

"No, *why*," said my son, "I don't know *why* he came out and left the door open."

"I thought you said it was a rock," asked my daughter, who was now lying down and close to sleeping. I nudged her over and scratched her back lightly. My son was staring at the phone and I could hear you breathing on the other end.

"He came out," you said, "because he needed to get into the light."

My son looked at me, then back at the phone.

"Okay, but why did he let them throw rocks at him? If he had a special Jesus power to open caves, why didn't he use that when he was tied to the cross? And just fly up?"

You were quiet for a moment and then you said,

"Well, that was a good question." Your end went silent again except for what was either the sound of you smoking or the result of you having smoked so much.

"Why did he let the bad guys hurt him?" asked my son.

"Because he wanted to live the life he set out to live. He wanted to show us about sacrifice and forgiveness, as the Son of God," you said. My son turned to me and his mouth dropped open. He picked up the phone and spoke directly into it a bit louder.

"Wait," he said, "God was, like, his dad?"

"Yes," you said, "yours, too. I mean, depending on how you

like to look at it. We're all loved by God that much. No matter what our powers or who our father is."

I hoped your voice would soak into their brain chips, my son being too young to remember this conversation and my daughter being nearly asleep. I didn't want them to discount prayer because some people sold it as a passport to an afterlife with vine gardens and a food court. I wanted them to feel freed by the mysteries of whatever doctrines they chose. As my children slept I looked at them and wondered who had taught you how to think, or perhaps how not to think.

I called you as my father was dying and you said, "Remember this: your dad is the most honorable man I have ever known." I held the phone to my dad's ear. I knew your voice, but the rhythm coming through the receiver was different. You were using another language with him and your tone was more strident. I suspected that you were passing along things the rest of us are not ready for, as my dad was nearly gone from this Earth and didn't need to wonder anymore, or wander. I looked to my brother and knew he was remembering the same thing. You there at the dinner table with us all those years ago, sipping your wine and laughing your big throaty laugh. Echoing our commitment to the unanswerable, the mysterious. Mystery is endangered but need not be extinct.

When I spoke to you recently you told me that you were getting married. Not to be inelegant, but what are you, late seventies? That gives me hope for all humanity. I haven't met your partner, Richard, but I can say he is a lucky man. It's because of you that I can go to any church and take whatever the service has to offer, all of it up for interpretation except kindness.

Dear Miss Girl,

(you) "Hey Miss Girl!"
(me) "Hey Miss Woman!"

Then, barely audible:

(you) "Hey Miss Thing!"
(me, even softer) "Hey Miss America!"
(you, only ants can hear) "Hey Fantasia!"

We bonded in about five minutes over lemonade and fries at the Chateau Marmont. Our shared devotion to skincare was only the cherry.

"Well, Hey, Miss P-Town!"
"Hey Miss Can't Find Me a Place to Park in Front of the Sunset Marquis!"

Miss Woman, you always greet me with a bright face on. Even when one of us is a tad suicidal we manage to laugh about something. I thought of you when I met that priest from Opus Dei, that sect of hard-core Catholics who believe to the seams of their Filene's Basement blazers that homosexuals will fry in a sweaty ring of Hell that has no TCM channel or Streisand. Miss Girl, I have to tell you that when this man asserted that "the only happy homosexual was a dead homosexual," I saw us rolling on the floor laughing just from sharing pictures of our hairdos from the eighties. This man said that homos usually commit suicide, and that there has never been a truly happy homosexual. I said, I don't know, have you ever seen Richard Simmons? He said, "Sadly Richard will be burning in Hell for all of eternity," and I said, "At least he'll be sweatin' to the oldies!"

When he narrowed his eyes and retorted, "I think you know what I mean," I was all sweetness back. "Sorry, but do you really mean *burn?*" I queried and he crossed his arms, said, "Yes, eternally," and I said, "Wow, so are you going to put them in space suits or something?" "I don't follow you," he said, and I was like, "I'm just saying, you better get flame-retardant pods to nestle those gays in, because *nothing?* can burn eternally without melting? not even a flip-flop, or one of those Japanese knives they sell on QVC?" His face was vermillion as he informed me, "There is another set of rules waiting for us in the Afterlife," and I said, "Oh goodie, can Poppycock be good for you? Can Twitter give you eczema?"

"Hey Miss Militant Gay-Lover!"
"Hey Hey Little Miss Flip-Flop!"
"Hey, Betty!"

Here's the thing, chicken wing. I know that as a homosexual born before the year 2000, at some point someone with a Bible or your lunch money said you were a sinner. Maybe they claimed to be quoting the American Psychiatric Association, which classified homosexuality as a mental disorder until 1973. If those party poopers had their way, you and I would have no drag shows to attend. Drag was looked upon like schizophrenia, which, to me? is some flimsy researching. Someone calling any of those drag queens crazy is bewildering, because when Miss Manischewitz sweeps out and takes our breath away, I can only think: How could a mental patient possibly mastermind a ball gown that also doubles as a deli case? And while we're at it, how on earth could a bunch of raging psychopaths keep a place like Fire Island so clean and crime free? It's really just finger pointing by a dangerous few who lack imagination and the keen ability to accessorize. We know that story, morning glory.

I grow misty when I realize you'll never know the homo husbands I lost in the eighties. Oh Miss Woman, you would have loved Hal— He could have sat and cried with us at *The Color Purple*, and his passion for exfoliating was on par with yours. Back in college we'd pack our T-zones with Queen Helene Mint Julep Masque and hang off the edge of the bed while the blood circulated to our olive green faces. We'd dangle there and he'd smoke while explaining Fosse to me, or Jesus, or the combo platter of both. Once the mask became hard we'd see who could make the other laugh to crack it. He died before he was even thirty, "off to meet my maker," as he said. I hope he got a big welcome party, with the disciples greeting him in footless tights with leg warmers and sweet tea. And Frank! You can take your Rambo's and 007's; if the apocalypse were approaching and Frank nearby, I'd have hid behind him. He could slay anyone with an actual fencing foil, or build a house from a hammer and some twine. He was Excalibur, Mercutio, and Robin Hood. Had he lived, he would have played every armor-wearing, sword-toting hero that enters on a horse and saves the day. I wish to God I could have seen that.

"Hey Cindy Lou Who!"
"Hey Ladybug!"
"Hey Miss I Cried at the Harvey Milk High School Awards!"
"Hey Kay Sedia!"

We'll be together in a week. I don't know what I will wear when we go to see our drag show. I'll think of you when I choose my shoes. I'll pick something in hopes that you'll say: Look at you, Miss Girl, don't you look pretty?

Nowadays, months can go by without any opportunity to even say hey there, but the last time we saw each other, you said I walked away and it occurred to you that I was someone always happy to see you. You knew I'd be at your side in a flash. What you'd been looking for in a boyfriend was not as important now that we were older. Sex was not hard to find, you thought, but the other stuff? Maybe it was right there, walking across the street in a Gucci trench, and you said

Why am I such a miserable cunt that I want more?
All the things I want and need are right there in her

It's true, Scarecrow. I've been in your own backyard all along.

Next week we are going to par-tay, we're going to have the kind of night where you come home still giggling when you're brushing your teeth. Before you fall asleep you'll check to see if the cute boy you met has sent you a text. When you pick up your phone it will be lit up to alert that someone is thinking of you at one thirty in the morning and when you click messages, there will be one and it will say

HEY MISS WOMAN

Dear Big Feet,

I never saw your eyes since they were closed, but your feet captured my attention. They poked out from under a sheet. I'm assuming they were wider than the norm because they seemed in proportion to their length, which obscured your face and an inch or so of afro above it. I have projected a lot onto those feet, not knowing anything about you other than the fact that you were a big deal on the basketball court. You may have been dreaming of life as an NBA star the day I spied you there. Obviously I don't know if you were a medium or big dreamer or if your mother did the dreaming for both of you. I don't know any of that.

I understand that everything I observed about your mother over those few days was colored by the fact that she was alone in a hospital waiting area. She sat on the couch like some rare species of sparrow, fine boned and immobile. I never saw anyone with her and I don't know how long she'd been there. My dad had just been moved to that floor of the hospital. He was recovering from brain surgery for a neurological disorder with the odd burlesque name of "tic douloureux." My dad got through every stage of his procedure without much drama. It went as well as brain surgery can go, but we stayed close by and were in and out of his room, the waiting room, and the cafeteria numerous times a day. It was one afternoon while making my way to the waiting room that I saw your feet and that little corner of your face, with doctors around you in a tableau that did not look promising. When I got to the waiting room I saw your mother perched there with her incurable stare. She was in that place where the high probability of failure intersects with a two percent chance of success. Hope at its most corrosive.

My mother and I started to fear for your mom, trying to ascertain what your status was based on how much she'd moved that day. I came in once and her gaze had lowered a bit so I went and sat beside her and asked

How is your boy

She didn't move or look at me, but there was graciousness in her tone when she said

He's just not so good

I didn't know how to respond but I was fairly sure that it would do her no favors if I were to burst into tears, so I said I was so sorry and went and found my mother. We stood there helplessly shaking our heads until my mom, ever full of grace, went and said to her, Won't you please let me get you a cup of coffee?

She gave the barest acknowledgment that she would accept that and then she went back to being marble.

When I returned the next day I peeked in to see my dad and then I darted over to look for those feet of yours. When I didn't see them I stopped a nurse and said, the boy, the tall one, where is he? It was a nurse I didn't recognize and she clearly didn't know that you were supposed to be a big basketball star and live to be eighty, she clearly knew none of that because she did not look up and said flatly that they had taken your body away.

That day was over twenty years ago. I've been witness to great tragedy since but I've never forgotten you. I created different details to your narrative to go along with what I knew and it never seems like what I assume is inaccurate. I feel like by having some understanding of your latitude I can deduce your center, like quantum gravity, which I can comprehend about as much as I can a mother burying her son, but if certain scientists are correct and it becomes possible to bend time, then I'll be able to ask you if any of my assumptions were correct. I don't need answers until then, unless the idea of God becomes willing to explain itself, in which case I am up for that Q&A. Where your story intersects mine is at my refusal to accept things too sad for me to process; my reimagining endings that haunt me. It's hard to reconcile that God is either entirely too secretive or has a totally deficient ability to prioritize. I hear people say, "It happened for a reason," or "It's part of God's plan," and I wish that made sense to me but it doesn't. I carry you around still and who knows why.

Perhaps there are no answers for us poor humans, but we know a handful of things. We know there exists a planet with four thousand versions of songbirds. Because that is possible and because on that same planet can exist sentient beings made up almost entirely of stardust, and because bonafide poetry erupts mightily from some of those beings, and there is music, sex, and babies that laugh in their sleep; because we are roaming a universe that may be a hologram, with another dimension consecutively projecting itself outside this construct of relativity and gravity; because of all that, there is no reason why my prayers shouldn't be able to reach your mother whose name I didn't even know. There is no reason why not, when nothing is completely harmonious with its description, not really, and there is a flaw in every theory of time and space.

From time to time I picture it. I see her watching while you go flying down that court. I see her shoulders moving almost imperceptibly to mimic your bobs and weaves around the other players. She is going where you go without thinking about it, tied to you, following and winning when you win, until you turn to wave and that puts her on her feet and beaming. I do know that if your mother is alive today she is thinking of you right this minute. I wonder what she prays for, and if you hear her.

Dear Former Boyfriend,

In July, we kissed until our lips were swollen, but by April I was giving dumb answers to your questions and we were fighting until we forgot our points. I don't remember having a single reasonable point, and you did, you had sound ones. I didn't know how to have an adult discussion, which I know was frustrating. I was frustrating, no denying it, but what was your point that weekend we argued all day and forgot to eat? We kept at it until we grew weak and unfocused, when finally you said, this is insanity, you're killing me, I want Mexican, let's go. I said yes, down with insanity, I just need shoes, and you said okay, but hear me when I say there is now a hole inside me that only salsa can fill. We made it outside into daylight, which was an adjustment, got onto your Harley and you yelled, Let's go to that place in Malibu, and I shouted back sounds great, but I think I just burned my leg on your exhaust pipe? You said oh, I'm sure they'll have Neosporin at the bar. We drove up the coast and pulled in, jumping off your bike and heading for the entrance, but the door was locked and the place was closed. You walked back to the bike and put your head in your hands, taking a deep breath and trying to fathom the unfairness of life, kind of how I imagine Moses looked when Pharaoh's magicians kept coldly one-upping him every time he thought he'd nailed it by, like, turning an umbrella into a boa constrictor, or how disappointed Mel Gibson looked on that poster for *Braveheart*. I put my hand on your back and said sorry, babe, I know you're starving. You said, voice cracking from the memory, that you'd only had half a Pop Tart and an Amstel Light twenty-three hours ago and now you felt like an outlaw. I said wow. I said don't cry. You said I'm not crying, goddammit. You gunned out of the parking lot grunting something that sounded like "strip mall." We rode another twenty minutes before pulling up to another restaurant as it was closing and when you realized the gruesome reality that they wouldn't stay open, you threw your helmet into the gravel and raised a fist to the gods. I'm starving, you bellowed, I could eat my bike! I need chips like I need oxygen! My kingdom for a chimichanga! I started to space out to avoid agitating you further and we got back on your bike and you roared, On to that dive downtown! I raced to put my helmet back on, but in my rush it ended up backward on my face like Ichabod Crane, and I was suddenly blind and could not breathe except for one eyehole that had landed near an open nasal passage. I didn't realign it for fear of being thrown from your Harley and I tried squeezing you and yelling over the wail of your bike that I needed air, but you thought I was being comforting and called out not to worry, the next place would have your combo plate or you would decapitate someone. As you slowed, pulling into the parking lot, I reached up to shift the helmet so I would not lose consciousness and gave a thumbs-up in victory when you cried out that God was on your side, they were open! I let out a muffled "hurlgraah!" from inside the helmet as you lurched forward into a parking spot, jerking me so violently that I stabbed myself in the shoulder with my thumb, but I was so happy to take off my helmet and see dimension in front of me, and shapes, that I did a kind of crippled sideways skip toward the restaurant. As we entered, the host looked at me with concern and said *buenas noches*, is señorita in fine shape tonight? He was staring at my hair, which had gone stiff from the wind and nearly horizontal from my body. I said *sí*, as you pulled me toward a table, and the waiter appeared and we ordered. I began to wonder what was sticking to my calf so I held a candle from the table to my leg and saw that my leg was stuck to my leg, the exhaust burn had grown to the size of a Kinder Egg. I said one sec babe and dragged my leg behind me to the bar, but couldn't remember the word for blister in Spanish. I managed to hit on something like *Mister, this old leg is hot and inside is the queso from that bike of my lover, help me hold the burn, thank you, mister,* which confused him, but then I put my leg on a stool and pointed, and the sight registered to the bartender, who was sympathetic. Minutes later I limped back with a tube of Neosporin in one hand while holding an ice pack to my leg with the other. You were now lucid, and I realized I was hungry too, but you'd eaten all the chips in the basket. I was getting light-headed from my flesh wound and from breaking the sound barrier on Ventura Highway when our food

arrived. You looked at my plate and said Beauty, you ordered
so well. You didn't glimpse at your own dinner as you dipped
into my guacamole. I eyed your plate. You had in front of you a
similar combo, including guacamole. I stopped moving entirely
and watched you dip a chip in my guacamole and say "What is
that but just altogether fucking yum." You weren't looking at me
as you continued to eat my food and I couldn't move from rage.
There was such a fog around me that I felt like I had entered a
Whitesnake video. I had a rush of leaving the physical plane and
I watched from the ceiling as I took my fork and stabbed you in
the hand that was reaching, again, toward the last of my guacamole. The fork made contact and stayed lodged in the fleshy part
at the top of your hand, the part they tell you to squeeze if you
have a migraine, and then I removed it and reentered my body. I
didn't feel recognizable human emotions, but knew my name and
could maybe quote some of the liner notes from *Bat Out of Hell*.
No one moved. You stared at your hand and said softly, whoa,
you drew blood. You leaned back and smiled. Babe, you said,
what did you do with that Neosporin? I said I must have lost it.
Go get more at the bar and could you order me some guacamole
while you are at it. You put your hand down the back of my shirt
as you got up and said my legs belonged in a museum. I smiled
but didn't look up yet because I knew that when I did I would
see someone who was a former and not a current, so I focused
on beer as I wiped the last little smidge of your blood off of my
fork and onto my napkin. I helped myself to your Negra Modelo
and thought about the lovely sound of the word *cerveza*, and how
much better things sound in a romance language, even when it's
only food. I looked down at my leg, realizing the scar would be

the second of two that I'd gotten that year. They would both be there in twenty years, like the faintest freckled mouse ears that really, you would need a map to find. It would take me almost until now to suspect that you were a good guy and I didn't even know you that well, or for that matter, a good many of the people attached to my scars, visible or not.

Dear Mentor,

Before you, I'd catch a fish from time to time, but I needed someone to show me how to bait my hook in this one way.

Most everything you said in the rehearsal room as a director was applicable to life. You said

Let go of what happened last time

And

Start with what you know

And

Don't expect a response

Our first week rehearsing together, we were outside on a break and you asked me what my character did at night when she couldn't sleep. I rattled off stuff I thought was super-interesting before I said, "and I feel like she's the kind of person who . . ."

I kept on, but something I'd said had given you a twitch. Your face was very close to mine and I remember the direction our bodies were facing in the courtyard, all of that. You put that one finger up, the index that you always gestured with by making those swirls in the air by your breastbone, like a kid swinging chewed-up gum around his finger, or the guy with headphones when you're on television signaling to you to WRAP IT UP. I don't know what that was about but I always found it endearing. Your fingers were small for a man, almost delicate, but your pirate's swarthy complexion and that long wavy dark hair gave you an air of exotic sensuality. Had I met you in Paris, or Florence, I'm sure I would have asked you if you spoke English before launching in.

You were nodding while I rambled and when I stopped you said

Uh huh? All that is good? But I would be careful of thinking about people as "kinds of people"?

I put my hand on that brick wall, just leaned there listening to you. It was humbling to hear a thing I thought I knew but really didn't. I didn't understand it in my bones yet, I couldn't honor it properly, because I'd never had it broken down by someone with that kind of authority. I only needed it explained once by you to be able to adopt it as some kind of anthem. As far as I was con-

cerned, you were holding a stone tablet and carrying a torch, reminding me that everyone is a mass of contradictions. There are
no "types" of people.

We had a lot of time together, relatively speaking. Years later
I was stuck and needed help, and I called you to come and watch
me. You were too ill to take the stairs backstage after the show, so
I met you at your seat. It took great effort to stand, but you did,
and said, I think I've solved your problem, because

*You keep saying you're hungry but there is a doughnut in front of you
and you don't eat it*

*You keep saying you're cold but you take off your coat and throw it on
the floor*

It was everything so basic and obvious that I'd categorically
overlooked. I wanted to kick myself but you inspired me, got me
excited to go strip away the baloney. I went back to the theater,
wiped the slate, and turned those simple needs on high. I took it
so far. I licked my fingers of every last trace of that doughnut and
sucked them off like they were a delicacy. I shook the napkin into
my mouth in case I missed any crumb, and I counted every penny
in my coin purse, double-checking pennies in case they were dirty
nickels, to see if I could buy one more doughnut. I buried myself
so deeply inside my coat to fight the chill that a third of my face
was obscured. I didn't take my hands from my pockets or get off
my chair until the room was warm, and when I took my coat off
it felt like breakthrough molting. Those notes were rudimentary,

but so rooted in survival that they gave me the inner velocity that allowed me to be perfectly still. I could hear my motor going, a car gunning in place.

You said things with such deceptive simplicity that they might have been easy to dismiss if someone less charismatic and substantive had explained them. Some things you said I may not have understood initially, or ever, but I believed you anyway. When it came to the theater you were anointed with indisputable divinity.

Michael came to visit you in the hospital and was taken aback to see you being wheeled into the ICU. He put his hand out and gently asked, "Are you all right?" You raised a brow and said, in that voice I could have poured on pancakes

Well, apparently not

In those days, intensive care was an immediate death sentence for any AIDS patient and that evening I guess there were a number of people in your room. Kevin and your mom were talking to the doctors, and Deb was there on your bed telling you things about the day so you could have someone to listen to and be less scared. She noticed that you had started to mimic her. A phrase like "Lillie is flying in from Texas" was repeated back as soon as she uttered it. She would say "Ralph pissed off a dog in the park" and you'd repeat it verbatim. You were parroting everything she said, and she was ragged and scared, and wondered why, why would you be sarcastic and torment her when there was clearly so little time left. She was fighting tears but tried to be calm and said why are you imitating me, is my talking upsetting you?

And you said, softly,

No. I'm trying to catch your rhythm. I want to catch your breath.

It occurred to you to take someone's tempo with you, since you'd be forced to let go of all hands at some point. You took the spaces with you. No way to take the voices you loved, they would have to stay behind, so you took the ellipses.

She sat there talking with you repeating, I think because you knew what might actually last. What you were allowed to keep.

Dear Young Leman,

"I think about why it stopped. Why you left and what was truth? What was blind passion, and I don't know, maybe the passion was the truth. Maybe the only thing that slipped away was the blind part."

That's what you wrote after we were done and put away.

You were right. Temporary blindness is useful. How can we see anything when we're so busy being seen? When we're being whipped up into those soft peaks.

It was sweet, being looked at by you. You were so young. We would spend hours calculating our age difference: "When I am Q you would still only be N and that will continue to suck," I'd say. "But wait!" you'd say, sitting up suddenly. "When I will be P, you will be M! That's not so terrible, right?" I'd try to picture it. "Maybe," I'd say, "but you still won't even have a yard. Or legitimate regrets. Do you even have your wisdom teeth?" You'd growl at me for ruining your idea. Threaten to bonk me with the champagne bottle. "Maybe when you're this many?" I'd hold up fingers to indicate. "But by then I'll be in a wheelchair."

"So what. I'll push you around," you'd lie back next to me, not needing to do anything other than roll over and put your hands behind the small of my back.

I flew you to Denmark and you showed up with a backpack and a Shakespeare textbook. It was good there. We looked the same in age so no one knew. We could fall on each other in the park or ravage each other by the elevator bank in the hotel, right there. "Going down," I said and you didn't look to see if someone might be getting off because you were busy getting off yourself and didn't care if we were caught. While you slammed into me I moaned too loudly, slid over, and pushed the call buttons with my hip. So used to hiding, a part of me wanted someone to catch us so I could say who cares. Who cares if I am hiding out in him, I thought. Go find your own dysfunction. Who cares if you loved me that well and you were that young. It wasn't against the law. Unlikely to make it another two months, I savored it. Binged on it. I thought go ahead, rip me open, and while you are at it, rip up my life's agenda into tiny pieces. It isn't working out so well anyway.

We went to the park after you got there because I wasn't working that day and it was warm out. Approaching the hotel we could see the flags in front slapping each other around. My skirt blew up and you caught it and held it down; a sweet gesture of chivalry from you who'd just put your fingers inside of me on a park bench, and there it was, in that second. That was the man you would be one day, holding down a woman's skirt in the wind, though by then you'd be able to buy drinks in any country. I knew in that instant I'd never know you as an older man, with reading glasses and a newspaper. That moment had been my glimpse. As we entered the hotel you said

Part of me would like to fuck you in a really expensive car and

Part of me would like to fuck you in a really cheap car

We lazed and read our books separately on the bed like two older people. I realize now that I was still terrifically young too, but you were so much younger.

Close to midnight we woke and took a taxi to a *Biergarten*. In the cab you went on about how we can't ever reach anything according to quantum physics; we can only really travel between two points. I said does that mean we have to walk once we get out of the taxi because I am tired from all the sex, and you said, no, listen, if I am here and you are there, I can come to you but it's only half the distance of our two beginning points, and I said, okay. That's far out? But I'm hungry. You can draw it for me later.

We'd sit and draw diagrams about the weather with stick people. At your mother's house during our second month of being improbable and nympho, she gave us watercolors and we sat painting the big wooden table she got in Finland when you were small. She showed me pictures of you when you were a baby and left us poems on our pillows when we stayed out late. I said, why are my feet always so cold here and she said, oh no, you have to do your socks this way, sit down, and she took off my shoes and socks and put them back on, her hands lingering over my feet, saying they looked like a dancer's. She patted me on the head when we sat together, even though I was taller. She liked me, gave me that beautiful Christmas ornament and said, well, I never had a daughter. I thought this was odd at first, but now that it's here in front of me, it seems, just . . . not at all odd.

We sat outside with our beer and pizza that went untouched because we couldn't eat knowing you'd leave tomorrow and I'd leave us after that. You asked me if I thought there was even the tiniest remote piece of me that thought we could keep going or be together again one day and I said yes. Then you said, well okay, is this just that thing, you know, where we aren't together but we will never really be happy with who we end up with, and I could not answer because I didn't want to lie a second time.

You left and we talked on the phone two nights later when I was in Ireland, or Belgium, I can't recall. We talked for two hours because for most of it you tried, do you remember doing this, for over half of that call, like an hour and a half of pleading, to get me to read the poem that I'd written you. I kept saying don't, they aren't meant to be performed, they're meant to be held and read with your eyes, I won't.

You begged until you were crying and I said stop. I said do you remember that time you said something like, you could fairly lose yourself weeping on my bosom, or some phrase like that, that was more iambic than organic? You sounded like a guy in tights with a bow and arrow. You said, yeah, that's me. Don't remember me like that though. I actually already grew past that and am mortally embarrassed that I said it, thank you very much. I said shut your face and I will read you a verse and you said I love you and I said shut your face. But I know you do. And you know everything,

I've told you before, okay, just listen and I will try. My voice was a little stiff at first but I started your poem.

On some word that offended or stung, you let out an enormous sob and I waited and listened and then I tried to make it better. We ended up fighting, but our fights never had any blows, really. It was mostly pleading and a bit of shouting. Someone laughing while blowing their nose at the very end and then sex, but that night we went back and forth until I was crying too, saying it's three in the morning here, I don't remember my time zone or what language to use to ask for coffee in the morning, I have to be in a corset in two hours, please, I beg you, quit it.

There was a letter waiting when I got home. The beginning was all about our future that didn't happen, with a little girl asking me questions, who was, you said, the daughter we would have.

The second half was stream of consciousness. You wrote all these possible scenarios, railing at time and sequence and all the things I'm tortured by now, and yes, I still have it. You made real sense in your spirals. The letter ended with you writing

this is my word howled to the moon and spat into the sewer, you listen, just listen to the street and the sky and you'll always hear me there because I caught you up close. I held you. good night

Dear Poetry Man,

When I got to my temporary apartment I'd barely finished counting the stains on the carpet when my phone started ringing. I thought it might be Søren so I dove for it. I remember his words precisely. He said he'd find someone with a car and get me in an hour when we would "go to the Starry Plough, have some beers, and listen to my friend sing so you can fall in love with him." He said after that we could all get on with life.

When we walked in there was only a small crowd. I vaguely remember a dart board, but what remains vivid is you. I'd never seen anything like you before, doing that dance that propelled you around the stage with your head and body tuned in and taking cues from two very different but harmonious rhythm sources. You were covering "Will It Go Round in Circles" and ripping it to shreds.

That song ended and you had a sip of beer and sat on the edge of the stage. You waved to Søren while I fought to look neutral because I was taken with you and slightly enraged for no reason. *Enraged* is the wrong word, but I felt like I wanted to kick you in the shins and then make you banana bread. I wanted to key your car and take you out for dim sum. It was admiration, passion and that voice of yours all mushing together and disarming me, making me want to smash something and kiss someone.

Meeting you in the parking lot after the show I told you I'd loved your version of "Feline." You were sweet, quieter than I expected. It was dark out but up close your eyes were as soulful as your voice. They were the ordinary blue you see countless times a day though hardly ever in a pair of eyes. The color brought to mind simple things—uniforms and buttons—but to see that color staring back was new. They weren't a color so much as an hour of the day.

Do you remember going back to your parents' house in Berkeley the next weekend and listening to music until the wee hours? We talked about poetry, and I didn't know so many guys who were into H.D. and Carolyn Forché. That was the night I sat on Søren's lit cigarette, which is, I mean, how or why did he leave it there, lit? I still remember how that burned and pretending it didn't hurt when we were kissing on that couch. On the way home I wanted to stop for a band-aid, but no one had any cash.

Eight years later you were playing to stadiums and I could now afford a first aid kit. I came home from shooting a music video and most of your band was in my hotel room with you, ordering extremely fancy champagne from room service. That night we dumped out all the candy from the minibar onto my bed at the Peninsula hotel and systematically ate it all while I listened to the horror stories of that one girl you were dating. I vowed to find you someone better as we fell asleep atop those empty Hershey wrappers. Years after that, on the day that a play I was doing was met with widespread hatred, you chased me around your hotel room in a robe reading a scathing review aloud while I held my hands over my ears. "Let's demystify it," you shouted, "it's better to hear it! This guy hates you so much it's almost funny!" Later while I sat crying on the couch you recounted the meanest attacks on your own work just to make me feel better. I almost got married to someone in your living room. And then I didn't a few days after that.

I won't forget you sensing I was about to lose it one night at a restaurant when things were not good. Let's get you out of here, you said, swooping me up and taking me all the way home. Most of all I see that narrow staircase to that apartment you rented by me when I was having a rough time. You literally moved around the corner. In the next couple of months you had to be away, you said, but you'd be home intermittently and wanted to be nearby if I needed anything.

That first day I stood at the bottom of the stairs and started up, knowing there was someone at the top who cared enough to move his endless pieces of stereo equipment, countless Playbills, and high-end cookware to a walk-up only steps away from me. I got to the top floor and you were moving stuff around. You said, hey did I ever burn you this bootleg of Rickie Lee Jones? You were holding a CD in one hand and a take-out menu in the other. Justin was there and he was leaning out the window, shouting at the delivery guy, "Are you Cozy Soup and Burg? No, I am coming down! Stay. Please." He stuck his head back in the window and saw me there, "Hey baby, can you believe it's snowing?"

"It's gorgeous," I said.

"Babe, I know you'll say you aren't hungry but we ordered for you anyway," said Justin, on his way down the stairs.

"Black and white shake, right?" you said, moving a speaker over so I could sit on it, "I figured I knew what you'd want." We sat by the window. Looking across the park, I realized that if it wasn't for one tiny square of a building, we could have waved at each other from our windows. We watched the snow and the people struggling to make it down MacDougal without slipping on the ice. The snow was still fairly pristine so no one was bitter about it yet. We sat there over ten years ago, no idea where we'd be now, but starting to grasp that we couldn't predict anything. We've been terrifically wrong about an awful lot but we did okay. We're still watching each other's dreams be dashed or actualized. Still saving each other a seat.

Dear Cerberus,

This is a once upon a time that happened too much.

I'm telling this grim tale to you three. You were the worst of those I called darling. There you are now, cowering. Well, *Konnichiwa!* Remember me?

I'm the gal who sat dumbly in a living room on the Upper East Side while one of your kind lifted me off the couch by my hair in the few seconds it took your wife to go fetch more pistachios. Didn't you. I put my fingertips to my scalp and they came away bloody as you whispered, "Keep your mouth shut about this." Didn't you.

Now don't be frightened. This isn't an indictment. This is addressed to you, yes, but also to myself, because guess who stood for it?

I don't believe in endings, happy or sad, so my relationships with you continue to this day. They are the kind of relationships you have with a pair of skis you know you'll never have to strap to yourself again. Maybe you never really liked skiing, but enjoyed being a person who could say, "Looks like I'll be hitting the slopes this weekend!" So you kept on even though it cost too much to get down a hill. Gave you windburn. I see nothing weird about keeping those skis in the basement. They offer a little nostalgia for crappier times. More importantly, they serve as a reminder that *I no longer have to ski.*

Wake up, please. I listened to you enough. I listened until I thought you made sense, which is saying a lot.

I can do anything now, from where I sit. I have five decades behind me, practically an elder, and I'm turning you into:

One mangy dog with three heads.

You are Cerberus, the three-headed dog who guarded the gates of Hell. I'm in this story, too! I get my own Disney soundtrack, coming to a speaker near you. You'll hear it whenever a hummingbird lands on me, or a dwarf ambles by hammered on Jägermeister. Rufus Wainwright can sing it if he is avail.

Don't pout. You'll still have a pack of fans. You'll appeal to those women who write letters to convicts in flowery script, affixing *good job!* and *nice try* ☺ stickers to their letters. They'll still call.

Get comfy. Curl up on your vintage gynecological chair with your flask or your cigar. You'll see yourself in one of the heads of this angry dog. You mistreated me. You know who you are.

There was a time and there was a girl she was funky and dreamy, with real baby fat and a wiggly mouth. Floating through the East Village, she was a muse waiting to happen.

She was I.

One afternoon I stopped on Spring Street for a soda break. I tugged at my tutu and looked across the way at an abandoned couch. There you sat, squinting. You didn't growl. You sniffed the air, acknowledging me with a head cock as I knelt down.

"Oh my goodness," I said. "You're so sweet!"

I tried to run my fingers through your coat but it was dreading on top. You needed someone. "Let's go back to my place," you said, putting your head in my lap. My head started to spin and you said

Please come back with me. When I'm not with you all I'll do is think of you

I moved into your cage that night. There was plenty of floor space for my routines, which delighted you. I discovered I had a gift for making you laugh. Sometimes my antics worked on the street and that was the best—you'd throw your head back in hysterics and pull me close, kissing my forehead. We looked like a candid photo from a tabloid with everyone staring. I felt famous. I'd always wanted to be that girl! The one with a dog so consumed with her that every passerby would take one look at us and want to go home and overdose. It was glorious; faces of all nationalities falling into the same mask of failure: *I'll never be loved like that*, they all seemed to say, while you pawed me.

One evening you came home with a pair of yellow stockings for me and I put them on and did a jig that made you howl. I was your favorite, you said. There was loads of time for me to read while you went to your therapist, who would call me privately to remind me to make your life more fun. "Smiles are contagious!" she advised. "Be his ticket to F-U-N! If you are gloomy it will only hurt you!" I said, "You can count on me, Doctor," and she said, "What?" and I said, "CAN DO, DOC!" She reminded me that she was clinically deaf and I should listen more than speak.

One night you called me to the office. Your eyes were icy. I started to do a time step but you said, honey, this is serious. I stood in the corner while you played back my answering machine. Any messages from dogs, which said, even, "Hey, I'm in town, call me," or "Hey, my house burned down, call me," or "Hey, this is the pharmacy, returning your call, call me," no matter what, you'd look at me and point to the machine until I said, "It's okay to erase that one," and you'd hit erase while we stood listening to those voices all high-pitched and jumbled as they ran away. I wondered why everyone sounded the same sped up like that, earnest and slightly hysterical, like cartoon mice planning a funeral. When you'd finished with that you patted me on the head and a second before the door slammed you shouted, "Be back later."

I went into the bedroom. My legs were quivering; I laid down, whispered "help." Lately I'd said my prayers standing up, before I got into bed. There was no time, once I crawled into bed with you. By then God was too busy. God was always closed.

Two weeks later you came back not speaking and wouldn't look at me. When we went out I tried to break up the bar fights and miscommunications with gas station attendants. I showed up at your favorite restaurant in a sassy new outfit: black leather vest and tight mustard-colored riding pants. Rickrack was sewn across each butt cheek like a parenthesis so you'd understand that my ass was always right in the middle of a thought. This seemed clever, and F-U-N, but you were L-I-V-I-D, dragged me to the bathroom by my hair. Pushing my nose to the mirror you said, "You look like a slut!" I said, "Ouch, my hair!" You barked, "Honey! You need to quit picking fights," but then you shoved your hand down my pants and said, "Don't get me wrong, you never looked hotter, but these pants are beneath you." You ripped them down and rammed inside me from behind as a woman came out of a stall and said, "Hey, aren't you that dog?" You snarled, "Lady, could we have some privacy, please?" "Oh sorry," she murmured, slipping out as you slipped out too and threw your sweater at me, muttering, "Cover yourself." You left me staring in the bathroom mirror, pants down. That's actually a swell game if you play it right, but this was not that.

I found my way to the table but there were only men there.

"Hey, weren't my friends coming?" I asked, and you pointed to my two girlfriends on the street outside the restaurant holding each other and crying. "The redhead didn't like men, I could feel it," you shrugged, "the blonde was just out of line."

I laid my head down on the table, eyes even with the dish of olive oil. I didn't need to look up. I knew the girls would come back, and they did, kneeling by your chair and asking for your forgiveness. I saw your hand on the lower back of one of them, moving in small squares. I had dry mouth. I said I was tired. No one heard me. I got up to go. No one said bye.

I walked home and marched to the office, took the top drawer out of your desk, and carried it with me to the bedroom without ceremony. I dumped it on the bed and started to go through every piece of paper. In about four seconds I thought, OH. I thought MY, I thought, DUH, I thought, OUCH.

There was a note from the salesgirl who'd sold you my yellow stockings telling you to wash them because they'd "gotten messy" when she modeled them for you in the dressing room. It seems you'd met a thirteen-year-old girl at the arcade? Her mother's lawyer wrote about complications from the plastic surgery you got her and there were nude pictures of her holding a stuffed gorilla. (Nudes were of the mother, not the daughter.) The dog-walker had written lovingly about your affair (this almost made me like you because she had a withered arm, which made you seem like an equal-opportunity misogynist), letters from a Dutch girl, a French girl, and a girl from the Yucatán peninsula, where you'd been last week when you said you had a charity thing. Ripped in half were photos of a blonde with you in Norway, sitting on a raft.

I was too weak to be angry and I could not get the theme song from "It's a Small World" out of my head. At least now I was cured of devotion, and phew to that. Phew.

You were at work when I left. I admit I took back my green sweater that you liked to wear, and my garlic press. As I ran onto the elevator your housekeeper dropped her hands at her sides sadly and said

Oh not you, too. I hoped this was different but they always leave crying.

Years later, you came a callin' Dog #2

There were whispers of your canine reputation but you seemed too good to be true. We went out at night, coming home and falling into bed with an eagerness that was embarrassing, both of us shocked by the comfort of the other's skin.

We wrapped in quilts and watched Looney Tunes. We ate fried fish sandwiches and did shots of tequila while soaking our feet in the kitchen sink. After two days the bed would look like a crime scene but we'd stay in until someone had the dentist or jury duty. I was covered in bruises and teeth marks, and your back looked like you'd been attacked by a raccoon. You wrote me letters when I napped and I woke to a crinkling sound when I turned my head, an envelope under my pillow.

Then your pack came to town.

Some quality male time was in order, you said. I cheered, go get 'em, tiger, and you said don't wait up, and I said, I won't, have a blast!

The next day I realized you'd slept through breakfast and then lunch. I was famished but you were disappointed when I ate without you so I waited, spacing out with a cat's cradle on the beanbag chair.

I snapped to it when a hissing sound came from your general area. It was like a radiator turning on, and your shoulders were twitching. I fell back, horrified. The neck of your bathrobe drew down and another black wet dog snout emerged, followed by new dog eyes and ears appearing in slo-mo. I gulped. An extra head lay on your pillow and it belonged to the mangy dog I'd escaped years before. Sitting up, both of you looked at me. The new head grinned at me and went flaccid. It hung there attached but only panting.

Was he your understudy? Were you so spent from a night of carousing that you had to call for second team? I didn't want to be rude, so I acted breezy and made a choice to ignore the bonus dog head.

"Do I have something in my eye?" I asked lightly.

"Come here. I don't have X-ray vision," you said.

I opened my eyes wide.

"Your eyes are fine, I see nothing." You laid back and adjusted your extra head without comment.

I tried not to stare but your eyes were different. They reminded me of the foam that comes in with the tide after an oil spill. Water combined with a compound not meant to marry anything clear. You sighed. You said last night was a throwback to the days when you worked the Underworld. "Those were some times." You sighed.

"I can believe it!" I said cheerfully, my stomach churning acid. "Hey, if I go to the drugstore do you need anything?"

"An extra toothbrush," you mumbled. I stopped at the door and turned. You were nearly asleep again but one of the new eyes winked at me, and the new snout whispered something in your ear, which put you in floods of tears. I couldn't make out every word, but you were sputtering about how we never did anything since I was always working and you never got enough respect. Bonus head mouthed the words "Blow me, chickadee" to me as you wept. I set about calming you, made you a grilled cheese and rubbed your feet until both of you drifted back to sleep, two heads snoring in stereo.

The next day I came in modeling my new parka. "Let's go to Dubai!" I jumped up and down holding first-class tickets and the hotel brochure, with photos of the indoor skiing school. I'd set it all up. "Cool," you said.

A week after we were back you both began to sulk. I scrambled for a solution.

"Who's up for a dude ranch?" I ran in dumping bags of cowboy boots, and fell in your lap. I flashed a picture of your own personal stallion, Digger. I'd set it all up. "Cool," you said.

In airport security on the way home you got wistful. You missed Digger.

"Who's ready for a week with holy men in India?" Bonus head yawned, but you swatted at him, said,

"Cool. Do I have to pay for anything?"

"Oh. Uh. You could tip the Sherpa?"

"How much is that?"

"We can sort it out."

"Cool. Can my mom come?"

On the way back from India you had a meltdown, saying you were always surrounded by my life. "I need to get back to my roots," you said. "I want my family to come visit." I said sure, but it was a challenge. Your brother pinched my sister's nipples on his way to the fridge, and your sister sat farting on my Civil War quilt, calling me a lousy feminist. She was correct, but still. Your mother said my aura was off and I should go in the closet and jump, to clear it, which I did, just as an excuse to get my circulation going since you'd been patrolling the thermostat. You required a cold temperature to paint your canvases, you said, or you would never connect to the chill in your soul. I said I bet you can access that chill even in a heat wave and you said don't get sassy with me, I said sorry but you haven't painted in months and my fingers are turning blue. I snuck into the living room one afternoon to turn up the heat but Bonus head ratted me out. Marching to the center of the room, you whistled. You clapped and stamped one foot and I hopped up, thinking, oh cool, square dancing! You were not interested in dancing, though, you were issuing an edict and you said

Everyone needs to remember at the end of the day that they are under my roof

This threw me because it was I who wrote the check for that roof and it cleared my bank.

You said

Who wears the pants in this family, who works harder than me?

I said I um. I said I do. I said please get out and that means cousins in the guest room, too. You said I'm leaving. I said, yes, you've been asked to. You said, I'm going and once I leave I'm not coming back, and I said yes, please pretend like it was your very own idea if you like, just shoo.

You said does this mean I can't go to Hawaii?

Years sped by, I had two wee ones of my own. Romantic love felt silly by comparison. I was useful.

One evening I made some tea and went into my den, and there you were. You were on your phone and when you saw me you waved excitedly. Putting your hand over the receiver you whispered, "One sec, I'm on with the president." You blew me a kiss.

"Who are you?" I asked.

You held up your hand and whispered, "Five more seconds, sorry!"

I took a sip of my tea. You definitely looked familiar, but I couldn't remember from where. You hung up your phone and sauntered over.

"I'm in such a different place now."

"From when? Do I know you?" I asked.

You put a finger to my lips to shush me and said, "I promise not to be fatuous."

It started to dawn on me. You were that guy. For years you would drift into my personal space and goose me. Yes! The guy with the vocabulary who did all the mean imitations that had people in stitches! We had taken a trip together? And then you had disappeared. Then we'd taken another trip together? And you'd disappeared again. I'd blocked most of it, but you seemed so nice now.

You made a pouty face and said, "I think we could pull it off: being married, kids, all of it. I rented a villa in Italy for your birthday and everything. I bid on it and got it. Go, or no?"

"I guess go?" I said.

There was a lentil in your front tooth. You leaned in, said, "This feels like home to me. The corner of carnal and home."

How strange, I thought. He sounds like someone wrote him. It would be like having a prosthetic arm that I didn't really need, or a toy vegetable garden.

We moved slowly. Appearances were made and you mingled beautifully. You could decorate and play backgammon. It all felt adult and you remembered to bring flowers and carry suitcases. There were weeks of disappearing but I was used to that.

Winter came. After five days of radio silence you blasted in smelling of gin. You were in a state. After hacking your ex-wife's email you discovered she was telling everyone you were a dog and that I needed to brush my hair. This time you were not letting go, you said. Face slick with sweat, you stormed to the bathroom and your shirt hit me in the face as you ripped it off and threw it. My view was partially blocked but in the mirror opposite the medicine cabinet, I saw them. I backed up in shock and nearly fainted. The two dog heads I'd disentangled myself from in years gone by were back. They hung from either side of your collarbone like shoulder pads with noses. I almost rolled my eyes. Three? Though maybe this was the answer? With better weight distribution and symmetry maybe you'd be the man I could count on? Or maybe I should call the cops? Now I understood why all the ascots. I was worried my little ones would wake and see you so I threw a towel around you and steered you to the bed. I tried to put my hand to your forehead to feel your temp but the other two heads snapped at me. Your eyes flew open as if you were remembering your cue and you stuck your tongue out at me, and said, "I want to say all roads are leading me pertinaciously to you but you don't do any social media." You belched. "Go pray, why don't you. Go meditate."

"Are you drunk?" I asked, but you were already sawing logs, the two auxiliary heads busy mapping out a game plan for how to best lick your testicles. I went out on the balcony, flabbergasted. My heart was throbbing from the shock but as I sat there, all the clues I'd ignored trickled in. The myriad things I'd let slide. I remembered then how terribly wrong it was, when, beast. I am sorry to call you out, but. You did. You cheated at laser tag.

I thought about that, and grew cold on the balcony.

I flashed on Head #3 throwing his birthday presents at me after opening the first one and saying that it was not what he'd wanted and

Did you even buy it yourself or just send someone to get it?

The image of Head #1 refusing to speak to my parents because they didn't order champagne to toast our engagement, they only hugged us and said congratulations and he said

How fucking hard is it to get a bottle and raise a glass and say something nice about me

And Head #2 calmly reminding me

If I raise my fist to you again just turn and go because if I start hitting you I may not stop

I'd said

But where will I go next time? I live here

One head had said

If I sit here on this couch any longer I'm worried I will kill you and kill myself

I didn't know who that was, that last one. I could see the face and knew the name but everything else was too hard to understand, so maybe I hadn't counted correctly and there were more. Maybe that was my problem—I couldn't count? Why else would I go hollow and take it? Why would I never call the pound? I said sorry so many times that I believed I was, but was I supposed to be sorry?

A ringing then, you were calling me on the phone, saying, I need you. I said okay but you seem really mad. You cleared your throat and said,

"Yeah. I think you are picking up on my resentment toward you."

Then began your *J'accuse*-athon, your attack on me for being rude to a man two years before. At the top of your lungs you shouted, but as me, shouting at the man. You were imitating me but doing the Korean soap opera version of it, as though I'd foamed at the mouth and clawed at his face; I was calling the man a motherf-er and throwing things at waiters. YOU HAVE TO BE KIND TO EVERYONE, you kept saying. Then all the heads were chiming in and attacking me, "Which one is this?" I said, and, "Wait, who's attacking me now? I can't even tell."

"You were so horrible to your nanny!" you screamed. The poor nanny could barely enjoy the massage I got her because my children were so demanding, you snarled, and so what if she cleared out my minibar. "The nanny deserves a drink at the end of the day!"

"Didn't you have sex with your kid's nanny?" I asked, "Like for months and months?"

There was a silence.

"That's different. I was at the bottom of my life."

Then you started on my children. We were a bunch of fakes, you said, with our going to church and meditating. You said your children couldn't believe how awful my kids were, which was when I started to hang up, but you began mimicking me again and I was fascinated as I realized, wow, that sounds exactly like your imitation of your ex-wife. *I am hearing a preview*, I thought. I've become an anecdote. He was trying it out on me first. I would be coming to a cocktail party near you, told between dinner and dessert. Convenient, too, since you were using the same voice for me and your ex-wife, you could just do a medley.

Then you, as me, yelled out a word that is not a word I have ever said, or a word my children even know. It rhymes with not smaller.

My stomach went tight and my eyes popped out of their sockets on springs.

I punched you in my mind so hard that you said ouch through the receiver. I stepped on the phone and ended you, walking out on your performance of me. I hung up on you, dog, for the last time. You cured me of overvaluing potential.

I have to admit also that having sex with you was like making snow angels under a rhino.

Bittersweet, my dove, though you must have known all things slow to a stop. The childhood scars of you are not for me to pinpoint and shave flat. Go to your local library and check out some after-school specials. Go to church. Line dancing, anything.

You didn't expect me to tell the whole truth, did you? No one would believe how mean you were. It would have seemed like a fable, which is only as effective as its moral, and I happen to have one of those, finally:

She woke up in Brooklyn and stretched. She went to the bodega to buy tangerines and an atlas. She strolled home at her own pace and checked on her pet geode. Turning up the volume on Sinatra, she bounced on the trampoline.

Look at that. She'd come to her own rescue.

She wrote stories and when she was low on words her daughter brought her some, carefully written on scraps of paper. Her son threw poems over rooftops. They laughed so hard that the downstairs neighbors poked at their ceiling with a broom. Warriors, all three of them.

One night she stopped by the window because of a shadow. She put on her glasses and peered out. Knelt there.

It was you, dog, and you were failing. You walked in a circle and lay on your side breathing smoke. Those two extra heads were shrunken and lost in your fur, now overgrown and gray. Oh lord, she thought, we're all just poor dogs in the end.

She called out and you lifted your head wearily, laid it back down between your paws. You were ashamed and she was too. She'd done enough bad things to be the beast in someone else's story.

She started very soft, just air at first, and sang. Her wee ones in their beds could hear her somewhere in their dreams. She went on until you were breathing evenly. You sat up, moving in under the tree and her heart caught on something when she saw you limp. It was a shock how old and broken you were.

"Lie down, beast," she said gently, and you did. When your eyes closed she inhaled deeply and told you this whole story. It went on until her eyes were little hyphens and her neck was stiff. It took a while but she knew that when you woke you'd crawl away forever, and then. She was I and I am older now and I am done. All over.

Oh, you are so tiny now. I can barely see you out there, beast. I don't need you anymore. Believe me when I say I am grateful for all of it. My aim was off, but true. Sleep tight, little monster.

Dear Rafiki Yangu,

How'd you get so happy?

Maybe you could always get everyone to join you on the dance floor, even when there is no dance floor.

Last Thanksgiving, we were all around that coffee table in the living room. Some people were on the rug, others in a heap on the couch. The kids got to stay up late. You played your adungu, the homemade Ugandan harp. Starting with a song in Swahili, you tried to get Hunter to join in, remember? He was too humble and wanted you to sing, but you wouldn't take no. You went on your knees, pleading, "Siiiing something, Hun-ter, siiiiing out, my brother . . ." Leaning across that table until you were up in his face, your singing dropped to a whisper and then rose to a howl. You sang that one line, entreating him to join you in Swahili, and then English, you lay down and sang it old and frail and jumped up and made it funky like James Brown. Hunter was holding his stomach, laughing so hard, and you'd both put back some Ugandan gin, I won't say how much. That was the highlight of the party. Everyone sprang to life despite being spent from all the pie and Thanksgiving haiku.

It could be that you've always had that pied piper thing, but your life took a hairpin turn when you were so young. I can't imagine there were any parties for a long time after that. There was too much to do.

When you threw down your weapon mid-battle you had to be quick, or the rebel army who kidnapped you might catch you. They would surely kill you in ways that would make you wish during your death that you'd never been born. What they did to escaped child soldiers is so far off the scale in terms of human atrocity that I can't believe I was alive anywhere drawing a safe breath while that was happening somewhere else. I can't hold those images in my consciousness and sustain the idea of a benevolent creator, but your faith does not waver. You believe in God.

You live as a free man now. "Free man" might be a relative term for some men, but not you. There is being kidnapped, brainwashed, and tortured, and there is escaping that. There is stowing away in a truck that you hope will bring you to safety, and when that truck is overtaken, the canisters of paraffin that you hide behind are pierced and the wax inside burns you so severely that your skin bleaches white. You are disfigured but it is temporary, more important that you run, and are free. You go looking for a distant relative who takes you in and gives you a mat to sleep on. There is a roof over your head and no gun acting as your pillow. You are free to work, and work is now freedom, even though you carry buckets through the slums for pittance and for more hours a day than most people are awake. Working your fingers raw is a privilege, because you have the sovereign right to be the boss and the slave, and you go back to school with your earnings and you graduate. Freedom is holding your diploma in your hands.

One morning you wake to hear that your hometown was taken over. People you knew, guys you went to school with were hacked up and set fire to, their bodies left to boil by the side of the road. You've already lost your beloved brother and now there are more children hiding, running. An idea comes to you that will bring massive work and responsibility but you don't hesitate. You will build a safe place for those children, a school, and you won't quit when reason tells you to.

It's been a cycle of having your arms tied only to liberate yourself again. This grew you an enormous wingspan to rise above the bitterness anyone would expect you to have. When your hands are tied now, it's not a surprise or an obstacle. Who needs more than a brain, and decency, you think. Wings.

Do you remember when we went to hear Adam sing? I couldn't stay because I had to be up the next morning at dawn to work. Watching you hear live music was so sweet that I would have stayed but you said no, you must go back to the hotel to sleep.

For some reason parking was easy but leaving was a pickle. Three parking attendants came out, each giving us different directions and each time we ended up somewhere we had to back out of. Getting out of the garage took so long that when we finally exited, people were starting to leave the show. I was agitated but at some point I grew mesmerized by you. You did not panic. It didn't even seem like you were suppressing frustration, you just didn't let it in. Each time there was another dead end you only got calmer, including when the parking attendants were downright rude to you. The only change in mood came when we were out on the street and you high-fived me, laughing and turning up the radio, saying, "Okay, give me a cigarette, please."

You are a reminder of how things could be if they were actually awful, and the unabashed face of joy when things are better than I realize. As I get older, things that were never interesting are alternately fascinating and thrilling. I'm sure that I never exclaimed over the grain of wood in a doorframe when I was in my twenties, or sat down to stare at a tree. I was afraid there would be a deficit of fun as I got older, but when I think of us being friends in twenty years, having pie on the porch while I beat you and Hunter at Rummikub, I don't know. That sounds pretty damn exciting to me.

Someone asked you about our relationship. You put your hand on my back and said

She and I share the same soul

Pretty sure I am not worthy of that but it's something I can strive for, having been already awarded it. I wish I could single-handedly support your school, but I am humbled that you trust me to help. I know you feel like a family member in our home and that is both an honor and really freaking lucky, because, who else can build a fort out of sticks with my kids, and who else jumps in my pool with me at midnight and then sits on the porch while the crickets harass each other and we play records. Talk about family and theater. Drink red tea with honey.

One night in California we were on the deck having a beer. I know there are things you don't like to remember but I wanted to know how you stayed positive. I asked if you ever got angry and you said, oh yes. You said, "When someone is bad to a child," and I said is that all, and you said, "Well, also if someone interferes with my performance on a stage." Then I asked you what you did when you felt so low about yourself that you couldn't go forward. You were silent long enough for me to think you might not respond and then you said

I go far out, maybe in a field somewhere quiet. I think of things I have done in my life that people tell me are good. I remember that I have done good

You've seen me be irascible and flawed and I don't fear you judging me, but I have worried you might do something so heinous that I'd be forced to erase you. It's entirely a product of my looking so far up to see you, knowing you occupy a place on earth higher than I will reach. In the past my doing that has been a fatal error. I forget that we are all made from ether and instinct. We're all missing parts and orbit the same moon.

I'm going to take you off that pedestal and I want to ask you to do something stupid right in front of me, so we can have that shock of human fallibility thing past us. I will look forward to that disappointment like I await next Thanksgiving, the day you now celebrate with us. You can help the kids to find branches for the thankfulness tree again and help Kenneth cut up paper for the haiku. I promise no more scavenger hunts, that was insanity, but if we need to have a break from all that, your gin will be waiting, and we can make dancing and singing mandatory.

Dear Firefighter,

As we crossed the street we saw you. You were covered in debris and white soot that flaked off of you with every weighted step. With all of those protective layers you loomed enormous, like a weary snowman trudging home from an apocalyptic winter. There was a buzz on the streets of downtown New York right after 9/11. Walking outside was like entering a comic book world with no gray area. There was only horror and heroes.

We'd taken duffel bags of steel-toed boots down to Ground Zero, walking home with nothing to say. You were trudging in the opposite direction, still wearing the remains of the World Trade Center on your body. Some people passing by held up a hand in acknowledgment or called out encouraging words. No cars were honking and there was no shouting to be heard for weeks after, it seemed.

That night it was still being called a rescue and everyone was holding on in a stasis, some people postponing what was too unbearable to process. I wonder how long you kept digging after you knew there was nothing left but buried screams to unearth. I try to imagine you alive today. Maybe you are? You are getting out of a taxi, or playing catch with your son. Writing a book.

About you: you weren't the only firefighter who made a stain on my memory. Six years later, I gathered my three-year-old son in my arms and marched down Sixth Avenue, sure that at Ladder 5 there would be someone to convince him that the small fire he'd seen across the street wasn't still going and perhaps on its way to swallow him. Ritchie was on duty, I said hello, and asked, "Has that little fire over by MacDougal been put out?" mouthing the word *scared* and pointing at my boy, who was still trembling. Ritchie kept his eyes on my son the whole time and calmed him down. He made him laugh and showed him how he'd brought the fire down. Did you have little boys like that come into your station, too? Come back the next day with their mom and bring you a batch of brownies when you were out on a call? Leave you a crayon picture, like my son did, and sit at attention for years whenever he heard a fire truck go by, searching each face aboard to see if he could recognize his friend?

You never had any next-day thank-you, or cookies waiting. I never knew your name, and your face I wouldn't recognize if I had only three to pick from, it was so thick with ash when I saw you. You didn't even look in my face as I saw you across the street and ran into your arms, but you saw me running and opened yours, lowering your head. Your eyes were closed, not weeping but not without weeping either and I rushed in, holding you tightly while your soot fell onto me like dandelion seed. I went on tiptoe to whisper to you while you nodded and answered back like we'd been talking for hours. It must have been impossible to tell from the outside who in our dance was leading who, or to hear that bell that rang for our ears only, telling us when to stop.

Dear NASA,

Sorry. I'm sorry for repeatedly stating that you were a massive misuse of tax dollars and basically an oversized playground for those who like to wear antigravity suits. I realize you haven't stopped the launching of shuttles on my behalf but I'm apologizing. Anyway, I didn't know what I was talking about.

Shamefully late, I began to understand that your research, directly and derivations thereof, resulted in: the artificial heart pump, the surface that protects the Golden Gate Bridge, the handheld jaws of life that save victims from car wrecks, and those invisible braces that Tom Cruise wore when no one knew there was anything wrong with his teeth. The FDA has you to thank for the drop in salmonella cases, as does everyone who got to read those charred Roman manuscripts from forever ago, A.D. Also anyone who rides a school bus in Chicago.

NASA, you were for me a bunch of geeks who lived on Hot Pockets and looked for E.T. while people on earth starved to death or couldn't afford health care or college. I get that this is asinine, that famine and an illiterate populace were not your fault. I am dim when it comes to a whole lot, but what I realized is that

Space is entirely poetic.

Listen. I read about stars that wander the galaxies. Some end up with their bright sides in the face of some dim unlocked planet who neglected to deal with its issues. With their volcanic air of refusal, those tidally locked stars never show their dark half and all the junk in their trunks where nothing grows. It is the baldest metaphor I can imagine. The white dwarf star, once so carefree, starts sucking the life force from its stingy blue companion, and a mutual thievery ensues until a supernova rolls up and obliterates everything they shared together. Somehow the white dwarf limps onward, meekly blinking, its space tag now reading, "Hi! My name is Zombie Star! Ask me about codependence!"

One Christmas I traveled somewhere with a sky that didn't stop. The night view of the planets would have made you weep. It was a romantic time and evenly divided; there were no scores kept. I loved someone who loved me back, that's all. We went far away to somewhere covered in snow, and the mountains outside our hotel window were magnificent and unscalable. As I recall it now, they seem glued there as a backdrop with no real world behind them. I question sometimes if I was taken there as a trick, since any proof I have of it existing is less than worthless. It can't be cashed in for anything but another battle. The view was not something you could take in properly without turning around to see where it began, so maybe there was someone behind it rotating one piece of scenery whenever I pivoted left or right? It was clearly too sweet and pure to be real so maybe someone painted it there, I don't know, but it was winter and I believed it because I'm a sucker for possibility.

On Christmas Eve we gave each other things and one gift was supposed to be something you couldn't hold in your hands. I had a poem for him, typed on plain white paper. Before he read it he wanted to give me my gift.

"Here, wear this, it's outside," he said, putting his coat over my shoulders. I followed him outside. It was fifteen below zero and the mountains and snow were maybe the most glorious I'll ever see, but up? That sky. It isn't worth grappling into metaphor.

He said to look up and he pointed, I wasn't sure at what. He said, "Do you see that one with the stem? Okay, to the right?" and then he said, "Now below, where there are three in a row, but one a bit off," and I did, and he said, "That one is, if you see it this way, it's an 'M'? Do you see that?" and I said, yes, I do see, and he said

It always will be there, in our lifetime, I will see it and that will be you above me, whenever I look up, forever

Would you have told me, NASA, what I know now, that the "M" is actually not? Would you have said that you have to look at things from the proper angle to give them a name? I'm glad now that I know what it actually is and glad I did not know then. I had that moment of believing that he and I were looking at the same thing. I know what the actual constellation is now and it wasn't me.

I don't know if you feel conflict when you hear the phrase "new reality," or if it makes you want to throw in the towel. When you realize that the only thing to be counted on is the shifting and reestablishing of proximity, do you ever feel like, *why did I bother searching in the first place?* We have to rewrite ourselves again and draw all new maps.

What burns off into the blank and what persists despite everything, is what I fall asleep wondering. Is there something? You must know something about the answer to that.

Of course you know the phenomenon with astronauts called "the overview effect," where the experience of seeing Earth from space can produce a kind of ecstasy. Apparently the view is so devastating from out there that the euphoria it induces alters you forever, and there is a scrambling within your brain to catch up. You can watch night wave across Earth from its baby beginning notes. A whole orchestra of arrivals and departures: imagine seeing Iowa disappear, when what surrounds it has been extinguished to black, or when the bodies of water on Earth are lit up to a blue that we can only guess at with our crayons and pens.

I wonder what they feel connected to when they are between the out there and here? Does it come with sound? I love the idea of watching the galaxy from far away and hearing being the same thing as remembering. Memory and fantasy could blend, coming in on clouds of song. Everything hard, all that earthly pain could be dumped out millions of miles away, becoming useful by feeding itself to the constellations. No shame, no need to be understood, just a floating about while listening to some entirely different and lasting kind of music.

Anyway I was wrong about you. I am listening with no small

amount of awe when you have more to tell us. Thank you, NASA, for keeping watch and realizing that our universe will never be anything but light-years new. I want to understand that, and I am so comforted by the fact that I can't. It only proves that some things won't allow themselves to be understood. They aren't for us to know and there's rapture in that, don't you think? Are you happy there, with your eyes glued to the heavens? You know so much, like why the ocean doesn't fall out of the sky, and that there is no upside down. There is no up.

Dear Mr. Cabdriver,

I don't think you saw me properly before I got into your cab or you would not have fought with me. That's what I want to believe. I think if you had gotten a better look then you wouldn't have been shocked by what I shouted, actually screamed, at you.

The address was not complicated. I was having you take me to a fairly well-known square. To take me to the front of my building was a risk that tested my patience and I had none. That day I just had none.

I had to go twenty blocks from home to complete something that would take about forty minutes, but I hadn't been leaving my house much. It took a lot of coaxing to get me to put on my coat and get out the door. I didn't want anyone to see me. Looking around to make sure there was no one watching, I got into your cab on my corner. You were magically waiting for me, which wasn't the luckiest thing that happened to you all day.

Once we were moving in traffic I felt I could take a breath. I spaced out and didn't pay attention once I told you where I wanted to go.

I don't know how long went by, it couldn't have been more than ten minutes but I looked up and saw that you seemed to be taking me in the exact wrong direction. I turned around and looked behind me, and to each side, to make sure I was correct. I looked down at the paper I was holding with the address and my expected arrival time, which was in five minutes.

"No," I said. "What are you doing? This is . . . no. You are going crosstown? Why are you doing that?" I held up the paper, even though you could not read it backward in the mirror. You did not look at me and pointed forward as though that was the correct choice. I stabbed at the paper as though my destination was there and not forward, and then I flopped back and hit the seat with my fist. I did this to keep from swearing but it did not keep me from swearing.

"Shit, goddamn. I mean, why, I mean why the hell-NO! Where are you going now? This is still wrong! Jesus, this is the wrong way too!" I waved the paper up and down, creating a whipping effect that did not soothe.

"Miss, do not to swear at me. You hear me?"

"But this is the wrong way, so why—"

"Miss, you do not to have to fucking swear. I am taking you. Miss, do you see?" You took your hands off the wheel entirely every time you said "Miss," finally turning up your music to drown me out, which only made you shout to be heard over it. I slammed into the side window as you swerved into a U-turn, which set us again in the wrong direction, and I slapped both sides of my face in disbelief. I began hitting the divider behind your head with my fists.

"Sir. Turn the COCK-A-FUCKING-ROUND. This is the wrong way and I need to be somewhere five minutes ago. I can't breathe. I can't. Wait. Are you fucking kidding me with the window? IT IS STUCK. OH MY GOD. Sir. I may barf. Open the fucking window before I barf. No, wait! No stop. No please. I beg of you to stop, STOP! That was Ninth Avenue, why did you not take it? Fuck's sake, why?"

"Miss, do not to yell at me, I am taking you!" You were now screaming so loud that your turban was shaking. You reached into the glove compartment and pulled out a map.

"God. Wait. NO. That, my friend, is a map of the United States of America. It is not going to help us. I mean, God. YOU NOODLE, JESUS. YOU CAN'T FIND CHELSEA ON A MAP OF THE UNITED STATES! Who gave you that? That person hates you, do you know that? He is your enemy. Just take me home." I tried to lie down in the backseat but sat right back up again, nauseous.

"No, I am not taking you home, Miss, I am to taking you to Chelsea." You were weaving in and out of traffic, and ran through a stoplight, barely missing a girl and her dog.

"You can't just—STOP! . . . LITTLE GIRL AND DOG, STOP! . . . Holy Mother, I asked you to take me home. Turn Around. Take FIFTH. Right HERE. TURN RIGHT. HERE. TAKE IT. TAKE IT TAKE IT TAKE IT. TAKE FIFTH. FUCKING TAKE FIFTH. TAKE IT. Yes. Thank you. Jesus.

Now turn right. NO, that is LEFT and I said RIGHT, okay, now stop. STOP. STOP THE MOTHERFUCKING CAB. STOP!" I had the door open before you were even a block from my apartment but it slammed shut again when I let go to dig in my purse for money. You muttered at me with your sitar music blaring as I threw a ten-dollar bill into the front seat and slid over very slowly, to the door. You turned off your music.

"Hurry up and get out of my cab, get out!" you shouted. I said

I can't hurry

"Go! I am not taking you to anywhere, you are very awful! I don't want you anymore." You were slapping the seat with your map, and waved it around in celebration of your being rid of me.

I was halfway out of the cab and stopped. I turned around, ungracefully, and I said hoarsely

No one does

My voice was shot and I barely got out

Look at me

You turned and looked, I think for the first time because you stopped waving your flag-map.

My life is worse than yours in this moment

I wailed

I am alone. Look, see? I am pregnant and alone. It hurts to even breathe.

Your hand slowly went to your mouth

I'm trying to get through it but I'm by myself every night and every morning and no one, nothing helps. I'm sorry I yelled. I can't get my shoes on anymore. Please, I know I am awful, it's been made clear but look at me, please

Look at me

I wasn't yelling. My voice was small. I wiped my mouth with the back of my hand and tried to decide if I should keep talking and then I said

No, don't. Really, you don't have to so why would you.

You made a gesture. I didn't know what it meant. It was a raising and dropping of your hands in your lap but I couldn't decrypt it and I got out and carefully closed your door, walking up the block, stopping to throw my piece of paper in the trash.

I don't know what you thought, if you had a daughter or a wife or if my little drama was a hangnail compared to your life. What I wish I could tell you is that I know it may have been. I don't know what had happened to you that morning, or that year, or when you were six. I didn't know your tragedy or hardship and it was grossly unfair of me to compare my life to yours. I am aware of my good fortune. What I don't have to struggle for that makes my life easier than most. I have thought of you and know you wouldn't remember me but I am sorry. Really, I don't fault you for anything except having that map of the United States of America in your taxi, which is about as useful as a walkie-talkie on the ground floor of the Empire State Building. The rest of it was simply a bad cab ride and every New Yorker has them. They're part of the landscape.

You were a living reminder of what I always professed to believe, that you never know what happened to someone that day, so try to cut some slack, but being bound by my own ropes I was unable to give you that. I realize now that whatever I was walking through was a part of my life, one piece of a bigger story that is mostly beautiful.

So, Mr. Cabdriver, I apologize for the profanity and the blame. I caused your turban to pop loose from its foundation and that was extreme. I maintain that your music was, to my ears, like a cat being declawed and I think you should not assume everyone can take it at that volume. That is a simple suggestion.

I am hoping by now you have GPS but I'll never know a thing about your life. I wonder all the time about the ceiling on what we actually know about anyone. This little moment from back then doesn't define that situation in time for me any more than it can for you. It was, in the end, much worse and more necessary than I would be willing to reveal, which is probably the most revealing thing I can say.

Dear Orderly,

I heard a deep voice. You appeared long enough to make annoying conversation and then tried to take my baby, dissolving before my eyes when I said no. I said, no, go. Or slept long enough for you to leave and come back. Or someone else did. I don't really know what I saw but it kept happening.

I was so tired, you see. I shivered with exhaustion, was blind with it. I'd pushed a person out. Out of an orifice that I challenge having been designated as the exit ramp for humankind. No matter how dilated. And forget anesthesia, I'd had nary an Advil. I remember thinking to myself, were I about to give birth, *It probably should hurt more than this.* So that's what you were dealing with. My pain threshold was not on that chart you were clutching while you pulsated in my sightline, discordantly calling out for me to hand over the baby, assuring me it was for my own good. I'm fine, I said, but you reappeared in your blue shower cap and booties, droning on

Give me the baby
Give me the baby it will be down the hall
With other given babies

I was tipped on my side to appear on guard. If I lay on my back I would fall asleep and I could not fall asleep because if I did you might take my baby. Standing upright was not an option. The two times I'd stood that day had resulted in an outpouring. My friend was standing in its pathway the first time and his lower half was drenched, "whoa," he said, "I mean, not since *Free Willy*." It was enough to fill a plastic pool. I could have swum laps in my afterbirth.

I realize I did not rest following the birth. I ate. I did that. I had a Big Mac but did not sleep. I followed that with a Quarter Pounder, two slices of pizza, a chocolate milkshake, no nap, and two cupcakes. Maybe three. It became night, late night, and the Antigone chorus of you insisted it would be better if you took the baby to the nursery. So I could sleep. But, I said, no my touch baby. I don't how am I tired. Care. Tired I am. How. No, I said. No touch him, please go.

You mumbled that I was making a big mistake but have it my way, and I thought, wait.

Yo, it's me, the woman drooling on herself, lying on my side like an odalisque with a broken vagina: I am speaking to you. My mouth can only manage "Go away, please," but my eyes are telling you the rest, all about a woman who has waited forever for this. Who wanted a baby since she was old enough to hold a toy of one. She was once a baby who wanted a baby, and now she,

I, yes, am very sleepy and unable to control reflexes. What does it really matter, though, if I just belched softly and consequently peed on myself? Yes, I am breathing so loudly through my mouth that I appear to be snoring with my eyes open and I smell. I am smelly. Look past that to the swaddled perfection in the bassinet. He vibrates with goodness and he is mine. You are correct that I am making a blunder but it's my mistake to make. And just you wait. This is nothing. I may put a fresh spin on ruinous parenting. I will undoubtedly scar him repeatedly, no matter how hard I try not to. I don't need help. I'm fully equipped to screw up my child all by myself and I promise I'll get right on it. Now in fact. *But in my own special ways that don't need your input.*

You probably have your own babies. Maybe you relinquished them to the nursery when they were born, anxious for a break. I respect the choice. I just don't know what is in that nursery, what he will hear, or if he might want me. It's possible, too, that if I didn't have seventeen maxi pads plastering my pubic area, and if there wasn't an inflatable plastic doughnut lodged under my ass and if my lady parts weren't swinging from where they struggle, tender and fragile as Tuesday's sashimi, if it weren't for that and for the high probability of pissing myself again or regurging a cupcake, I might consider cruising over and checking out that nursery. I really can't though, and don't want to risk him being over there alone and having a sucky and lonely first night on earth. You don't have to understand. I lie here in the curious and mystical position of not caring what anyone thinks about me, maybe for the first time in my life. I care only about the little body wiggling in that plastic bassinet.

If you see that little baby next to me, you will notice he's not an ordinary child, despite all the ways in which he is stunningly, exceptionally ordinary. There will be much celebrating of his average-ness, by me, and his below average too. He won't be able to jump until he is almost eight, will not be capable of pronouncing the letter *r*, and will pass through a period, as his mother did, where he will stutter so badly that it makes him cry. There will be plenty that he won't be the best at, but it is within all the medium and below that I will find relief, knowing he can enjoy the enviable position of normal, and the thrill of improving from floundering to adequate. I will also get permission from his average to marvel at his extraordinary. He will bring home his poetry notebook from school, his poems an unintelligible mass of spoken dialogue and exclamation points, but then one day he will produce poem after poem that would have made Whitman himself cry. There will be plenty of difficult and even intolerable, but he will burst forth intermittently with a grasp of humanity so unshakable and deep that I'll remember the infant who stared back at me in his first moments. He will struggle with his homework until he rips the paper in despair, but then suddenly out of the sky will fall fully realized ideas and phrases, flowing from him with such force that he can't stop writing, can't be coaxed to stop and when he finally puts down his pencil he will have a tiny blister on his finger. I'll know the boy who earned that blister, because I saw him in our first hello.

When I have the energy I'm going to drag my body around to study him up close again. I hope I won't set off the call button or accidentally kick a bedpan to the floor, and apologize in advance if I do, but I need to see him again; his too-big feet, that overbite, the brow knit in an anti-expression with which not a blessed thing can interfere. The wash of eternal over his gunmetal eyes will seem like something that has existed forever, and is only now beginning again. I'm pretty sure they call that holy.

I won't have much to say. Most was said in our first moment, when we were so quiet. He swam through the air to me and there was nothing.

There was nothing between us. No spaces.

I suppose it was the first moment I was thoroughly alive because I fell too far in it to ever describe it. There was nothing to look at because I was too busy seeing, and I got to be a beginner too. Will always be now, as every moment with your child will never repeat itself with something lovely after it, like a sunset or a passage in a book. Real time with them, I think, is the only actual. Everything left over is just a weather report.

This morning, before I got here and he was born, I wrote to him in his yellow book that I kept for recording thoughts. I said

You are on your way I just wanted to say OW WOW that was you banging on the door so you will be here soon should I say bon voyage?

I closed the book and sat waiting for that pain that dovetailed its wrenching ecstasy. I put my hands on my stomach and went straight toward it. It was the sort of pain that I can handle, and when it passed I leaned over and scrawled in that book again, I wrote

I hope I do okay by you

and

please, let's like each other

I will clarify something so you don't get the wrong idea. My own mother. She came to see me in a play in college and spent the entire day beaming at me in the background to not distract or steal focus. Waiting shyly whenever I floated over, she gave me her sweet smile and the batting of her eyelashes that calms. When I burst into her hotel room sobbing at midnight, she sat up and put her hand to her heart in alarm, her ladies' hairdo protected by a silk sleeping bonnet. "What is it, dear, what's wrong," she whispered so as not to wake my father, who was already half dressed, assuming there was a bomb scare or a tornado. "Sweetheart, what?" she said, patting the bed beside her, too modest to get up in her nightgown.

"I'm so sorry, Mother. I'm awful. Happy birthday. I forgot." I put my head on her shoulder and wept. She just laughed and patted me.

"Oh, honey, no. You had too much going on, don't cry."

My mother asks for nothing. My mother does not ever swear or comment negatively of others except with a light rolling of her eyes. She said to me as she watched me with my infant son, the best compliment I have ever received, in fact, she said

You are the best mother.

My dear, you are better than me.

You should have had six more.

Anyway I won't match that. She let all of her children leave the nest without making it about herself for one moment, and how she managed all those partings I can't fathom.

So you see, sir, I know what kind of mother you might take me for, based on my not giving up the baby. You probably think I'll be the smothering kind. I really don't think so. I've been aware, since that first hello, of the inevitable good-bye that follows it. Actually begins on the heels of it. If nothing else, it's my job to prepare both of us for those farewells. I want so deeply for him to celebrate his freedom. A couple of tugs at his heart when I leave him at college or wherever, but I am hoping he feels it his ethical imperative to go and have fun without the thought of Mom lingering. I will have practiced the good-bye in the mirror, meditated for days before it happens and will give him that moment of being a little sad and then *forgetting about me entirely.* And I am crafty! I will have tools to help! I'll have the movies we are going to make, the horror movies and music videos, the home movies that go on longer than any polite person could feign interest, of him sitting in his high chair in the bathroom while I do a shimmy, shimmy and then two spit takes in the sink while he shrieks with laughter every time, like I am Chaplin, enough to fill a whole memory card, or the movies of us going cross-country in an RV and him in the front seat with a lime popsicle, trying to incite truckers to blast their horns by waving at them in his surfer shorts, shirtless, his skin perfect and unmarred as the smile he gives when he turns to the camera, thrilled that the trucker waved back! I will watch the quiet films of the three of us back when we would have Monet Day, where we'd fill the bathtub with cheap flowers from the deli and food dye that we'd drip around them, huddling on the bathroom floor and painting what we saw. I can pore over all the Post-its he's left by my desk, with "I love you mom." "But I love you." "I do." "This is the thing, I love you mother." I'll have the memories of him showing concern over every old person on the street who walks alone. Him helping white-haired ladies down the street, or holding the door for so many people in the morning at school that I worry he'll never get in the door himself, and that time he said Mary-Louise, Mar-la-weez Mar-la the beautiful, Mar-la beautiful, that's it, Mommy, I will call you Mar-la beautiful. I will call you that forever, until my bones are air.

I'll remember him dozing off, being close to dreams and then waking with a start and whispering, please sing me a song, Mom. I will remember all that in private when he is gone. If I am the best ever, I'll be happy when days go by and he forgets to call and then calls and says it's because he's been doing something wonderful, and like my own mother, I'll be thrilled to hear it, whatever it is, and his not calling me won't be touched on. This is what I am shooting for. It will take massive effort but I can see it. I can picture myself doing it right.

Look at him there, would you? I mean, have you ever? I almost can't believe it. He's my only and my one. He's my ever and after. Sorry, sir. It may be the very best choice, but no, you may not have this baby tonight. He is my job now, the best one I've ever had, by a zillion, and I will be doing this one until I drop, in my own way and I say no.

I haven't even heard it yet. The sound that will make me happy to have been born, the sound I will draw on when I can't breathe or think straight, when I lose or fail, the sound of a small voice looking for me, or looking to be sure of me when I am right there, the sound of

mommy?

I have that coming. It will make me taller, brighter, better. Put everything in its proper order of importance.

Dear Storyteller,

I feel I've lost thirty friends in losing you. It's like an entire region wiped out: Yoda, Hercules, Santa Claus, and the Scarecrow, Atticus Finch. You were the real-life version of every one.

You would tell me

Don't you dare let go of that, you must never let anyone take that

And

All we ever owe each other is the truth

You flew so high, and with such regularity, where the rest of us are mostly earthbound.

We told each other everything already. There is no need to write to you, I just wanted to see you in these pages, despite the fact that I can't put you into words. You mean something untranslatable.

Now I can't imagine an afterlife that doesn't include you describing life and death. I can't wait to hear it. It will keep unfolding the more I consider it, like all of your stories. Its ending will I guess be the meaning of life? With you unwrapping it, certainly it will be something bigger and more phenomenally wonderful than simple human happiness. It will be continued. Like you.

Dear Uncle,

You never occurred to me. I didn't imagine you or consider the sacrifice of someone like you until I saw your name on a document. It said "guardian." Still in shock from that word, I looked again and saw "siblings," with other names unpronounceable to me, and I sat and rethought my fantasy. My potential daughter has a family? Who is alive? What will that make me? I could only envision her rejecting me one day once she understood that I was just a second chance at being provided for; a white, Western woman who didn't speak Amharic and couldn't make injera. My dream was a baby found in a field, left by a door, or fallen from the sky, not a little girl who'd been held and loved. Given a name and a birth order. I imagined that baby born to a mother who couldn't provide for her, but I never realized I didn't want to picture that woman or her family. I assumed I would find my little girl only desperate for my arms, but yours held her before mine.

You carried her to the orphanage. You walked with her on your hip until you got a ride hours away to that small brick building, strung with barbed wire and guarded by men in uniform. There is no way to know exactly who you handed her to when you felt her skin brush yours for the last time and no recording of your last words, if you spoke them with her crying in the background. That my daughter cried I am certain. I have the photographs taken moments after you left and the tears hadn't yet dried or stopped falling. I know the sound of her cry because it met me when I walked into the orphanage and heard a single voice wailing with a kind of hopelessness you usually only hear in an adult, someone with no expectation of being saved.

I heard that cry and fairly floated up the stairs to follow it despite my heavy bags, and as I passed a woman in the hall she pointed in the direction of the sound and murmured something I understood only by tone. It was my baby crying. They'd brought her over to be waiting for me instead of leaving her with the other babies and she was alone and terrified. There was such resolve in her wailing, and she quieted so immediately when I knelt in front of her that I can only believe she thought she was being left a third time. Knowing my daughter now, and who she is, I know that the tears in the photograph and look of hallucinatory disbelief on her face are proof of who you were to her. If she hadn't trusted you and needed you, she would have been easy to distract when you left and I watched the nurses at the orphanage make a ballet of their soothing. I wonder what you said to her when you took her away from the hut, or where she thought you were going when you set out to walk a distance that I might complain about if I had to travel to in a car. You wanted to give her a chance and you gave her away, believing she would get it.

When I went to meet you, we sat in a courtyard and spoke through a translator. You had brought along your children, her cousins. It would have been simpler for you to make that trip by yourself without those children, three of them under the age of ten. There must have been something you wanted them to be reassured of in meeting me.

As we sat down across from each other under that tree, I realized one of the many things that day that made me rethink my actual level of sensitivity. The first one was that we had a shared point of confusion: I had never occurred to you either. That is to say, I never occurred to you as I am. You turned to the translator and asked him

Where is her husband?

You were looking behind me for the father you'd envisioned. He told me what you said and my throat went dry. I flashed through the events of the last four years and felt wildly unsuccessful at life. I said

I don't know. I mean, I just don't have. One of those.

I tried to look friendly and like someone you would entrust with a human life. Your hands were clasped in your lap, the children next to you, stiff with fear from meeting someone who could only appear like a woman who'd just stepped off of a spaceship. All of you looked at the translator and then slowly started to look at me in longer glances, but when I brought forth the photo album I'd brought to show you where she would live and sleep and play, the children avoided my eyes again. I was taking their cousin to live on Mars, with things as concretely alien as beds with sheets, toys, and carpeting. A crib with a mobile of a cow hanging over it must have looked like an Escher painting, though they had never seen paint, and paper was extremely rare.

The agency said to have my questions ready for you because it would be overwhelming, so I had prepared three. The last question was really two, and both so profound that I felt my voice failing me as I asked you about your highest hopes for her, and your gravest fear.

I hope that she will be taken care of, go to school and perhaps one day be something, a doctor.

I fear that she will not know God.

There are so many reductive adjectives used to describe those materially less fortunate, words the privileged use to anoint them. Words like *proud*, or *graceful*. "They are such an elegant people." "The women have such a regal bearing." It never rings true. Having seen what I saw when you brought me to the hut where my daughter was born, and introduced me to the people in your village, I felt like I was hovering over every judgment of my reality and yours, unable to land. None of the families I met were intact, everyone had lost children, parents, or a spouse. There was not enough of anything for anyone. The only bounty was in categories of suffering or possible ways to die. I didn't feel them looking at me with distance, they all smiled and shook my hand. I hid my embarrassment at how stupid I felt when I entered your hut and was alarmed by the darkness that swallowed me despite it being late morning. Of course I knew there was no electricity, no light would be there except for what might creep in through that ceiling of straw. I knew it, but I couldn't fathom it until I stood inside with you and stared at an actual nothingness and my eyes adjusted to near black. There is nothing, and there is not one bloody thing. As you pointed at different parts of the hut that were designated for the cows to sleep, or the spot where your family of twelve eats when there is food, or where you slept, I saw spots with absolutely nothing in them. There was an absence of comment on your situation that made you seem twenty feet tall. It's something I could never know if I hadn't stood there, with you showing me what life is like on another planet where there is no complaining, or showing disappointment.

You were kind. I don't want to quantify or describe it to anyone who won't see how far you walk or what you have to eat or where you go to pray. It feels vulgar to be more explicit about what you face. I saw your life, less than lucky in every obvious respect, but blessed in ways I'm not built to understand. I don't think you would appreciate being characterized as anything other than a man who loves God and tries to be good. I think I know what actual divinity is because you handed it to me when I said I hoped I would come back and you would meet my son, and you said

You must, because we are all a family now

I hit a new threshold of speechlessness when you gave me the most tremendous gift I've ever received and then thanked me. What can you say to that, there is no saying, "Oh no, thank *you*." There's nothing but commonality. Just humility and being keenly aware that I will never live up to that gift, but will wake up every morning and try ferociously to meet it and marvel at it.

Dear Lifeline,

The day you married my friend, I pulled up to the hotel and found you outside in the driveway giving directions to someone looking for the check-in.

I waved, rolling down my window, and you loped over with a huge grin on your face. You folded your six-foot-four frame through the car window to kiss me hello and I said, how is she, where is she, and your face lit up as you put one hand in the air and one on your heart, and you said, "Oh, you can't believe, she's in there weeping. All day, like this," you said, drawing a stream of tears down your face with one long finger and making a mime's expression of anguish, "she's just been crying."

I put a hand on my heart, too, as you reenacted her anguish. You were beaming at the thought of your lovely bride, tears over-flowing on the morning of her wedding.

I asked could I go and find her and you said, "Are you kid-ding? She's dying to see you. She will probably see you and pass out from crying again. It's epic, I mean, pure Chekhov. She's amazing."

I rolled up my window and you did a little soft-shoe move and waved me off with genuine exhilaration in your eyes. I thought, gee, that's something I haven't seen before, a man who could find beauty in a woman's unruly display of emotion. There was no making her tears about you; just tap-dancing in the driveway and accepting that you were about to marry someone who was spilling over with feeling and too honest to conceal it.

The wedding was lovely and simple, except for one moment. Your bride reached the aisle, which was just around fifteen feet of grass leading to you. Still on the verge of weeping, she stopped. We all turned to face her, expecting her to sweep by, but she was planted, staring back at everyone. It's the moment where everyone is rooting for a woman's beauty, projecting loveliness onto her even if she's low on it, but my friend wasn't doing that production. She crept up those first few rows until she'd taken a soul count of every person bearing witness to what you were about to swear to each other. Her brow was set and her eyes fervently searched the crowd, her face aching with sincerity. If any part of me was somewhere else I was snapped to the present; she wanted to fully inhabit the moment most people say they barely remember.

I called you one night, nine years after that wedding. I don't know if I needed someone to hear me or talk to me. I'd stood outside many cold nights in a row that month after my kids were asleep. Sometimes I'd dial a friend only to hang up before they answered. I didn't feel like anyone wanted to hear me complain and I had nothing terrific to report.

I stood on the tiny balcony of the absurdly overpriced sublet that was draining me of enormous amounts of money. I looked at the lights in Battery Park. I could see inside people's apartments across the street, families decorating Christmas trees or sitting on their couches, watching television together. I thought about all the places I'd lived, which were too many to count and how at one point in my life this apartment would have felt like a palace. I moved the phone to my other hand so I could warm that one in my pocket for a second. I found myself dialing you. My nose was so cold that I had to keep rubbing it to revive feeling in the tip. You answered.

I said I just wanted to talk. You said great. I'm listening.

I said my kids are asleep and tonight I just waited for them to go to sleep so that I could have a drink.

You said okay.

You said what else.

I said well, I was never a big drinker before, isn't that enough, and you said, I don't know is it?

I said it's too dark here, where I'm sitting. I really hate my life and there are reasons why. Some of the reasons I can't bring myself to say, but here are some and I started listing. Their combined weight made me nauseous while I listened to myself. I felt charged, opening up, but it wasn't all that pleasant. I hadn't talked to a grown-up about anything real for days, and worried I might be rambling.

I said I have to get it together, I'm a mother, this isn't good enough, and you said, okay, good enough for what? I said my kids. You said you're an amazing mother. I said I wasn't this morning, and you said *you make a very good case against yourself, it's incredibly convincing*

I said what do you mean and you said, what I just heard is you putting yourself on trial and assuring me that you're guilty of an awful lot. It's like you're talking from a script you've written, do you know what I mean, and I said yeah but I have no new material.

How do I fix myself, I asked. We talked a long time, with Lady Liberty shining over there to remind me why my sublet was priced so high.

It's risky when you call someone in that state. When I left my daughter's village in Ethiopia I needed to talk to someone. The experience was so unhinging that I felt drugged, my head was bobbing around as I replayed it all, and I rested the side of my face against the car window and asked if we could stop to buy a phone card so I could call the States. When my father answered I just started talking. I only have eleven minutes on this phone, I said, and he called to my mother to pick up the other line. They listened so beautifully. My mother with her gentle amazement and my father who was so present, I wish there was a word for impossibly present; there was no small talk from him, no perfunctory exclamations. In every silence I knew he understood. I knew the expression on his face after we hung up. He would lie in bed that night and think of nothing else. It sounds like a small thing but it was fathomless, how connected I felt to him during that call. I knew I'd never be the same again after what I'd seen that day and I needed a particular pitch of listening and he hit it. He met me there fresh and followed, voice full of emotion. There was none of me alone while I stood on that dirt road in Africa, the Bale monkeys jumping through the trees above my head.

I remember your voice that night. You were so sane and male, and I needed a man's voice. You said two things, you said "you need to lay off yourself, just for a day, can you do that?" I said maybe, I'll try and you said, yes try. Then you said to do you a favor and write down some things that are good and send them to you. You said you did that every morning before you got out of bed, you'd lie there, "clearing the cobwebs out" and ridding yourself of grudges. Ending wars you were ready to fight, mostly against yourself. I said how come some people do this to themselves and you said hey, I get halfway through every day and I want to blow my fucking brains out. I want to drive off a bridge. I can taste the bitterness when it seeps across my tongue, making me feel dry and unlucky. I'm telling you, you said, I just want to break something, but then I ask myself

What can I do? How can I be of service to someone or to this moment, what can I do to help

You said, what the hell, who doesn't understand self-loathing? You have to get it out, even as a joke. Stuffing it all the time makes you explode later, and who doesn't understand feeling really hopeless? Seriously fuck anyone who doesn't understand, you said, everyone gets to feel bad.

I get that you don't fully know how great a man you are. I know enough of what you do in the course of a day to be massively impressed. You are a good husband and father and you don't put yourself first, which makes you fairly rare. Despite your never advertising it I've discovered how honorable you are. You started fighting self-destruction around the age when most guys are hitting impressive levels of indulging it. It sounds like you went through the kind of stuff when you were a kid that a lot of people use as an excuse their entire lives. They whip it out like a get out of jail card, the fact that they had to endure this or didn't get enough of that. From you, though, I keep noticing a lack of blame.

I said okay, now that I've laid out the ugliness in me you'll never have an impure thought about me again, and you said fuck no, I'm having one right now. I asked you about my friend I said how is she I wish I could visit her; I miss her. You said you know what? That woman? She'd go into battle for you. She loves you so much and so do I, so you have that going for you.

I said thank you. I will try not to, I said, but if I need to, can I—

You didn't make me say the word you said, yes call, please, that actually helps me. It's good for me. Call. I said okay. I hate it when I have nothing positive to say and you said, "Fuck, I hope that doesn't hold for me because if I call you and just leave a message saying, hey it's me, I hate myself so much right now, are you gonna, what? Hang up on me and say that guy's weak?" I said please, and you said I didn't think so, go write that list. I said thanks, really, I'll talk to you later and you said sleep tight, I'll leave my phone on.

Dear Neighbor,

"What I do is, I take the thing."

"The honeycomb?"

"Sure, the honeycomb."

"How big?" I ask you.

"I don't know, like," you hold your rough laborer's hands about six inches apart from each other to show me, "about like this, and I dip it in the jar of honey. I hold the comb in the air so they find me."

"Wow. Okay. And then you . . . what?"

We are sitting on my screened-in porch. You are looking past that tree, to where the quarry is.

"I go where the worker goes, and sometimes I might start a little fire."

"With what? How big?"

"Matches, it don't matter, just . . . small, you know. The bee flies away from the smoke toward the hive." You shrug. "Sometimes I throw a little flour on them so they are easy to spot?"

"Okay. Then you, what, catch it?"

"The worker? No, hold on." You hold up one finger. "I follow the smoke, because the bee makes a line, a straight one, and I follow it."

I slap the pillows on the daybed where I am sitting. "Shut up. You follow it? Where?" I am laughing because I can't believe you actually do this and that you know how. You are laughing, too. You are leaning forward, hitting your knee with your fist and you laugh so hard that you take off your hat. You put your hand on your stomach and take a breath.

"Aw, jeez, well, the worker." I am still giggling a little. "Stop," you say, "you're going to start me going again. Anyway, the bee gorges itself on honey and I follow it awhile until I lose it. I mark the spot and come back and repeat the whole thing all over. Can you believe it? I must seem real simple to you."

"Not simple," I say, shaking my head in true amazement. "You are like a freaking Grizzly Adams. So when does it end?"

"Well, that depends, see it's just—" You stop, giving me a look like you are sorry I have to listen. "Do you really want to hear this?"

"Are you out of your mind," I say. "Look at me, this is better than *Gone with the Wind*, I am riveted."

You take off your hat and rub your eyes. You have been up since four this morning and fed all the animals. Already been to town to check on one of your job sites.

"Aw, I can't be that interesting, you're just being nice," you say.

I stick out my tongue and say come on, finish, what happens to the beeeeeeeee.

"Okay, well, I have to tell you, last week," your voice drops to a whisper, "I ended up in an abandoned house because the hive was in the wall!" You end with a shout, like the wall was the punch line, and I am laughing too, but not completely sure why.

I make you tell me the whole thing; how you found the house and what the owners said when you told them you wanted to buy not the house, but that one wall. Tearing it down yourself, you raked in about thirty pounds of wild honey. Real wild honey, not what you buy at the store that says "wild honey," but isn't wild at all.

"I gave them a tub of it too, them owners, and they were so stinkin' happy." You take a sip of coffee.

"You did not!" I say. "That's . . . wow. You are off the charts." You shrug. "Can I heat that up?" I point to his coffee.

"No, I'm good, I'll take another one of these, though, if you got any?" You hold up the last corner of a muffin, a little sheepishly, and I hop up, giving you the stop sign so you'll pause the story until I come back. I take three steps and come back for your coffee anyway. "I'll get you a new one," I say, taking the cup. "You want jam?"

"Heck no, your muffins don't need no jam, girl." You touch the top of the large iron crucifix on the bench next to you. "That's real pretty," you say, more to the cross than to me.

I go in the kitchen and start the steamer for the milk. Out the enormous back window in my kitchen there are trees painted on the sky in more shades of green than I realized existed four years ago. You taught us the names of those trees and paid my kids a dollar when you tested them and they were correct about which was which. That's just one chapter of country life you opened up to us. The pages of our index before you were mostly empty.

"Oh, thank you," you say, as I hand you the muffin, which is steaming from my warming it. "Will you look at that. You spoil me. I don't deserve this."

"I put in molasses and almond meal," I say, wishing we could spoil you as much as you do us. We try to refrain from calling you, but the fireplace, the carpenter ants, someone got a suspicious bite; so many things seem to occur outside my wheelhouse and you are fluent in the languages of trees and bugs. Wood. You never let me feel like we're a bother, and partly that's because of your wife, who greets us with hugs in our communal garden or a wave from her front door. She steps out mid-conversation, with her thick red hair shining and her constant coffee mug: "They said you had a thing going on with your sink?" Or "Did you get the garlic we left in the barn?" She knows country life has endless moving parts to keep in order. She tells me about books she's reading, and I give her an apple pie when she brings us the poppy seed bread her daughter just made. "Still hot!" She says, "You can't believe how good, taste it, you'll want to shoot me for bringing it."

When your pond freezes over we bundle up and the kids put on skates. Your son teaches them hockey with you lying down on the ice in front of the net to catch the puck. We make a bonfire in the tepee that smokes so furiously your wife and I can't stay in there without tearing up. The kids roast marshmallows and stay up too late. When I go in later to make sure they are sleeping soundly, one of them will have a stripe of marshmallow still spackled across their chin.

"They won't ever forget these times," you say, and I know you're right. Sometimes I worry we are like the bees you tell me

about. The kids are always swarming around you, a constant
drone of "When can you tie the sleds to the four-wheeler and pull
us?" or "Will you jump in the pond?"

You make gallons of wild honey each year and collect it yourself, despite being allergic to bees. "Aw, I just wear a suit," you
say. The wild hives that you track are a whole process. It can take
days, with you baiting and following the worker twenty feet at a
time.

"Once I track the hive they lead me to, I find the queen. She's
easy to spot, because she's tall like you, and moves to different
music. It's like she's listening to jazz while the workers are on
their heavy metal." You laugh and shake your head. "Pretty
dumb, right? I don't know, they been doin' it for thousands of
years though, and that's why they say 'a beeline,' that's where that
comes from."

"So you find the tree with the hive and then what do you do?"
I ask. "Chop it down?"

"Aw no, I just mark it," you mime carving your initials in a
tree, "and then it's mine." You shrug again.

"And that's it?" I wonder how you keep track of all your trees.

"That's it. I don't do nothin' with it. It's just I had the patience
to go that distance. The honey stays. This is just so, I don't know.
I can find quiet, and follow through with something. Me and the
trees, you know."

"Okay," I say, trying to imagine myself spending that kind of
time to find something, only to leave it with a mark. To carve that
moment into a length of bark that someone might run their fingers
over one day, wondering who I was.

When my friends come to visit, they are mystified. They love that your friends just wander in and out, like Uncle Charlie with his many stories, who is not your uncle, and Papa Bob with his endless energy, who is not your papa.

"Jesus," said my friend Debra, "it's so familial. Maybe you can be cousin Zsa Zsa." She ran her hand over the wall of your root cellar and marveled at the fact that you built it yourself from scraps of metal and brick you saved from a worksite. No one can believe that you make everything and share it with people you've just met. When you come in to say hello, you give her bottles of maple syrup and little bags of garlic from the garden. It's always Christmas, you say.

Later on I'm puttering around making cookies and I almost don't hear you knock. When I go to the front screen door I see you on the other side of it, holding up a six-foot black snake.

"Look who I found," you say, lifting the snake by the neck. "I was coming up your front steps and he was on his way right to you."

I shriek. You caught my snake, or actually, you caught the one I saw and now you have him captive.

"You're a snake charmer too?" I ask him.

"Oh, stop," you shoo me away, but like any man, you are happy to be the one who caught something he was chasing, and like certain women, I am happy for a man to find something that was about to hurt me and grab it by the neck.

I step out and touch the snake. He is so black that he shines green in the light. Coming closer I see he has bits of yellow. "Isn't he a beauty?" you say.

"That's the one," I say. "How did you know he was coming for us?" Yesterday the babysitter called you because we saw him in the driveway. She turned white as a sheet and body-blocked me from going to take his picture. I wanted to see if it was listed in the poisonous category, but she'd screamed like a lunatic and pulled at me, stuttering that "They fly, some of them! No, really, I'm so for sure some fly! Like, into your face, fly!"

You were over in two seconds on your four-wheeler with a rifle. Ready to slay the flying snake that I think the babysitter had confused with the cartoon of the squirrel, because as you pointed out, they don't fly. You couldn't find the snake but came back the next day because, well, you weren't sure why, but there he was. You must have been tuned in to that frequency that doesn't display on my XM.

"Sometimes I just get a feeling," you say, shrugging, which turns out to be an adorable gesture when one is holding a six-foot snake. It occurs to me that you've been through enough in your life to not be daunted by a serpent. Losing your two-year-old son to a drowning accident you said put you low enough to shake the devil's hand, and you won't be venturing that way again. That kind of grief must make a snake look silly.

"Is he poisonous?" I ask. Rendered powerless, its attack face looked a little desperate, like it would be willing to cut a deal.

"Nah, he's afraid of you. Sure he'll attack, but only if threatened. He's important 'round here though. Kills the mice. Listen, though, you might want to think about cutting this maple down. If there's a storm it's gonna fall on your roof."

I look at the tree. It doesn't yield much syrup anymore but I still hate to fall it.

"Are we tapping on Valentine's Day this year?" I ask.

"Yes indeed," you said. "Are you still my assistant?"

I nod. "I live to hang those buckets," I say. The sound of syrup doing its *plunk-plunk* and *plinkity-ploink* is an orchestral drumbeat that brings me a kind of quiet. It's like a bizarre meditation to sit and listen. The first day you taught me to hang a bucket and drill into a maple, you waited until you'd found the perfect spot and made me sit there, eyes closed. I was surrounded by the sound of sweet draining from trees and falling on century-old tin.

"That's a music you don't hear in the city," you told me. I opened my eyes after a few minutes and gave you the thumbs-up. The sun moved out from behind the clouds and you looked up. "Now do like this," you'd said, taking my chin and turning it into the sunlight, saying, "Close your eyes again," and I did and you asked, "You feel that? You feel that warmth on your face?" I said I did, and you said

That's the hand of God there, touching you

We will probably hang a couple hundred buckets this winter. Last year I spent too much time making lunch for everyone and trying to get the kids' snow boots on and off. This year I don't want to miss it. We ride around in your pickup and tap trees for folks who have maples on their property but can't tap themselves. We ride with the windows open listening to The Bridge on Sirius XM while the buckets slap against the side of your truck. I come home worn out and feeling like a regular pioneer, someone who could churn butter.

Right now I watch you climb back into your truck. You wave and shout over the engine. Thanking me for the morning, you say

I learn so much when you are listening, thank you

I wave and go onto my porch. I look across the creek where my new barn will be. I count the sugar maples in my yard and watch you grow smaller as you leave slowly down the hill, driving with your one free hand while out the open truck window the long black snake hangs, swaying.

Dear Gem,

Your goat-face is such a map of sweetness. When you chew on my son's shirt or look at me through the pen window that perma-smile is so Christ-like that I have to fall to my knees and hug your neck. I pat your giant hairy belly with little slaps, releasing clouds of dust from your gray coat. When you were little I could hold you in my arms but now it takes both my daughter and I pushing with all our might to shove you back into the barn.

You have to know that it is entirely because of my loyalty to you that I was willing to castrate another goat.

This wasn't a mutiny on gonads. My readiness to hack off Bully's testes was my instinct to protect you and I was ready to get after it.

I want to be clear: Bully was only doing what biology asks of him. When a goat wakes to discover his scrotum coursing with blood, he starts butting into trees, silos, and the UPS woman. Bully had not been dehorned and he sported a set that could do real harm, not to mention that he was a breeder. Shortly after bringing him into the pack we had three baby goats. I know you had no hand in that, Gem, since you have neither horns nor a nutsack situation that makes you seek quality time with Peaches or Melissa. Bully may as well have moved into the pen with an open bar and a Commodores cover band playing twenty-four/seven. He strutted around bleating to himself. He took long naps during which he let forth farts that were just to the left of geothermal. His vibe was equal parts entitled and misunderstood, leaving a pen of ravaged lady goats that huddled together and licked their privates. The gals appeared both sated and needy, like they wanted to open up but needed therapy. It was hard to watch. I'd open the pen to find them panting, looking like they'd give up their feed ration for a tube of Vagisil.

Bully, I speak to you directly now. I saw you bang those lady goats from here to Xanadu and sometimes you weren't even in the mood. As you hammered away at Diana Ross, I'd see you distracted by a chipmunk. I'd see you looking around like

Is this really all there is?

Gem, you know it was your needs I was addressing in having to unsex your friend Bully. He came with massive swinging balls and pointy horns. He used those horns on you, Gem, gentleman goat, and that is where I drew the line.

I won't forget the sight of you, Gemini, as you rounded the corner that morning while I exited the pen after collecting eggs. To see your face bloodied and cut by the horns of your goat-bro was too much. When Bully trotted up moments later, I was still wiping blood from your beard and his eyes were cold and dead.

He rolled up like Caligula, mid-assassination.

Bloody skin tissue dripped off his horns and onto a nearby chicken, who tried to flee by frantically jumping into the pen with the piglets. This created a gruesome, live horror showcase of *Babe: Pig in the City*. I ran to my neighbor gesturing wildly for him to turn off his table saw, and he looked stricken when I told him about the attack on you, Gem. He marched into his barn and got the castrating pliers and we stopped to get his handyman Louis to help us.

Now, I have held down a girl goat to clip her horns or shave her ladytown privates before birthing. It isn't easy. You need two sets of hands for that unless you tie them to a post, but holding down Bully was another ball of wax. I had to sit on him. I sat on Bully and thrashed to and fro as my neighbor gripped his horns and Louis lay on the ground with both arms around his hind legs. This part was merely to get him into the pen so we could figure out the next step.

Gem, I may be projecting, but you bleated and Bully seemed to answer you. He slowed to a stop except for the clump of blood and facial ligament tissue swinging from his forehead.

What did you say to him, Gem? Did you say "Bro, you don't need balls to have balls?" Whatever it was, Bully heard it. He looked at the girl goats on the hay with flies buzzing all around, knowing he was expected to cruise over and bang each and every one. It was a job he was not up for, because he turned back to me with a plaintive expression that said

Lady, I am so ready for you to take this off my plate

My neighbor stopped and we read each other's mind. He got the other pliers and dehorned Bully. This was the loudest and craziest experience of my adult life, bloody and insane. It left your friend Bully with a few more years of goat love but unable to harm you, Gem. It calmed him down sufficiently.

Last week we had to move Bully to the back pen by the pigs since the ladies are expecting again. You are there, Gem, keeping watch on the mamas-to-be and it's a job you couldn't be more right for. Sweet granddaddy goat, that's more how I see you. You were never meant to be a baby daddy, or a player, and there isn't a drop of shame to be found in that.

Dear Little Owl,

You are nothing yet, in the absolute best way, and I am your eyes since yours haven't opened. You've not even met air! Or purple! Or snow. Or your mother, who is my friend! She is lying here so ready to hatch you. Embarrassment is years away! Ditto candy and kissing. Falcons, punch lines, and regret are even further down the road, with certain agonies that I hope never appear.

I tell you this now before you can speak: strength is a myth. It's not what it is, when it looks like what it is. It's usually what it is when it looks like something else. It takes bravery to admit that you're petrified and keep soldiering on despite it. Oh, and, "easy"? Also a hoax! If it existed it would be sold for the same as what you got it for—nothing! Ha!

Gather perseverance, perspicacity, and Pez. Be wary of guilty pleasures. Best to open the floodgates and let pleasure wash over you until you're floating in its yummy, with not a wink to guilt.

Try saving guilt for having gossiped or disappointed your children. Be sheepish about not reading Proust or neglecting to offer your car at the right moment, or your kidney. Don't tell lies. Lying will slowly set your soul on "decay," unless you really and truly must lie, in which case LIE YOUR EYEBALLS OFF, lie until your nose grows so long it touches the floor when you drop your head in shame, but then go seek forgiveness.

It's terrifically useful to recognize where you are lacking in relation to others. Accept and even celebrate it because envy will poison, it will give you acid reflux and strange pervasive malodors. I believe you will know, when the time comes, about Colorado, the Beatles, and the high road. About keeping secret your good deeds and giving when you don't have enough set aside for yourself. I know that you'll find and be found.

And I know that you are coming! Any second! I'm next to your mother on her birth slab! But Holy Moses what do I hear from yon auxiliary power dock? I recognize this song from its opening notes, and wow. No, I can't let this happen. I won't live with myself if this song, which is seeping into your delivery room like atomic sewage, is allowed to continue. I feel conflicted to interrupt this C-section as my dear friend's uterus is being traded hand to hand like a Frisbee in a game of Ultimate. She lies there beatifically in a blue shower bonnet, unaware, but so help me, the song is still playing and you are about to come out, *into your one life*, and I'll be a monkey's uncle before I stand by and let the first music you hear be "XXX is a XX." I get a sudden image of you hearing it and clutching the umbilical cord, hurriedly zip lining straight back into the womb, traumatized, so I politely but firmly ask the nurse, please, sir, I realize you have other shrimp to fry but it's sort of an ethical imperative right now that I have the iPod remote. I'm so sorry but this song is not worthy of the moment so by all means keep sterilizing that thingy but could you please point? Nurse points to it! I'm now diving for the remote, heroically changing it in the nick of time, and great day but if it isn't Bob Marley! All sunshine and feral joy spinning out, and then . . . Lots of muttering and orders given over there where the doctors are with your mother and then so fast! You are found!

Like royalty you are held up there in a moment that doesn't need anything but observance. You are here. Here for all of us to wonder at and dream for. It isn't even love I feel looking at you, still dripping and swimming, but something higher.

I go to where they've laid you to measure and your father is there. He is standing over you to the side swaying a little, hands behind his back about a foot away. He is not touching you, not even reaching, and I see his eyes burrow back and deep. He knows this moment is escaping all of us and he is suspended inside it. In the hall before they let us in the delivery room, where we were standing just an hour ago, he'd said,

this is my fourth child, and this, this next bit here

then he made a gesture with his hand as though dividing everything on earth in half, as if to mean: this is what matters and this is chaos, and he said

this right now, this is the only time I am all here and no part of me needs time travel

Right now I see him standing over you, still not touching. I see him out of his time capsule and connected to the immediate and the Ever of you, which is all the gravity he needs.

Then he hands you to me, little owl. I have you. I hold all your new and your ancient. I carry you to your mother. She holds you. I sit. I watch that happen.

Dear Doctor,

I came to you only partially conscious. Once I went into shock you were already saving me with your vast knowledge that I will never grasp. I'm confident I wouldn't understand the most basic medical strategy if it were explained to me by Mr. Rogers.

I went to sleep feeling poorly and woke at two a.m. with a pressure on my left side so intense that I put my hand over my mouth to muffle a cry. I searched the Internet for "agony on the left side of the body" and read that you only needed to be alarmed when vomiting blood, and as if on cue I coughed up something too salty to be saliva. I went to the sink and what I expectorated was pale pink, which I thought qualified as only blood-y? I tried going back to bed but my mouth began filling with blood, and three more times in twenty minutes the color of what came up deepened from pink lemonade to beets. The children's nanny answered her phone but I don't remember much after that until she arrived. I was writhing while my son urged her to call 911 and my daughter curled up in a terrified ball at the end of my bed. The paramedics arrived and when they came into the room, my kids stood up. My son put his arm around his sister. He tipped forward at the waist in my direction as though he were decorating the bow of a ship. He was craning toward me with all his might while she had crawled so far inside herself that her face would have seemed impassive if not for the set of her jaw. Her eyes patently demanded I not leave her, *don't you dare, I won't let you* they said, blinking fiercely. The imprint of them trying to look like their own ideas of dutiful children for my sake is the one I took with me. No matter how far I drifted I saw them there like that. When I pictured it in my head the image vibrated a little, like looking through a viewfinder.

As you know, I almost wasn't here anymore. Do people feel grateful for almost dying? I felt oddly privileged, despite seeing everyone poised to go down another set of tracks while I was held forcibly behind.

For weeks I had felt unwell but the doctor said it was just a cold so I kept going. At night a terror would crawl across my neck and up my arms. There was a prescient thought so horrifying, a voice saying that I was not entirely safe. This voice was ghoulish, it made me nearly roll my eyes, but if I was alone or anywhere silence could tag me I'd begin to actually tremble. I worried. Ignored it. Pet the dog. Snuck a cigarette.

That one Saturday I seemed fine. I went upstairs and sat on my bed. I noticed that I was breathing quickly.

I took off my shoes, looked at the chair in the corner, and considered moving it. I shrugged in response to nothing.

There was a mirror across from where I sat and I saw my reflection, which I did not like. I didn't look right. There was nothing to recognize except the names for things: brown hair—check, black coat—check, haunted expression—check, but I couldn't understand how my name went with that face staring back. I remembered buying the mirror, I saw myself years before in vintage boots, wandering an antiques fair in another country. Who was that? Why was I talking about peaches and champagne? Was that me in the memory or was this me, here, and why did I feel like both were doomed? I went cold inside. A rushing happened, but it eludes me how to describe the climate of your entire life's experience catching up to you and presenting itself. I felt myself at nine years old. At thirteen and thirty-nine. At fifty. It all entered my body and I swayed, drunkenly, though I'd only had coffee. It happened on my inhalation, and I was simultaneously elated and petrified to let go my breath.

My head began to shake back and forth slowly in answer to the question I hadn't realized I'd asked, which was *what if I died, I feel like I might*

I turned away from the mirror, my head saying no to myself, shaking back and forth. That feels awful, so no. I looked over and saw my soundless refusal staring back in that mirror.

You don't get to clean off your desk. You don't get to say I prefer April. It can always be tomorrow morning. The severing is complete and cauterizes all autonomy with it, which yes, is obvious, but not fully grasped until you've heard the sound of machines and voices keeping you alive, and then imagined the absence of that sound, so unceremonious when it quits. When I woke up in the hospital where it nearly happened, I saw the room as it would have looked had I died in it. I lay there listening to the swill of oxygen tanks, the ensemble of alarms and beeps, and I imagined the whole orchestration abruptly stopping and everyone in the room filing out. I saw the overlit hallway where my friends would have stood while you explained what happened. I knew the face of at least one of the men who would have put my body in a bag and zipped it up, and I could picture that bag being taken through the back doors of the hospital. My friend Nikki was wearing her blue T-shirt with the arrow on it when she dropped everything and left her children to go to the airport. I have an image of her returning home in the same T-shirt. In my mind every scene is dressed with the actual props and wardrobe, making it seem like I escaped something I was already in the midst of. The fantasy stops once I get to the point of my children being told that the last time they saw me was the last time they ever would. That image of them in the morning when I was taken away by ambulance, when they stood there so courageously, has to end with them in my bedroom.

Seeing it play out with an unhappy ending distills a life span to no more than the inexorable velocity demanded of working organs. What is it like in the room when they shut down? Is it like the hitting of a light switch, which is just an interruption of current? After you turn the switch, photons remain clinging to the walls for a disputable length of time after our brains tell us that it's dark, and what if we hovered there like that, part of us painted on surfaces in an in-between state. This could be true if we are nothing more than the future beds for violets and moles. Where did I go when I went into shock and started speaking in gibberish? I felt myself convulsing and came out of it long enough to see my children's nanny cover her mouth and cry. I strained to put my head up, saying, "Don't worry, please, I always shake like this when I'm afraid." I asked about this later but everyone in the room said that I was not speaking English. Unintelligible sounds fell from my mouth. *Metabolic encephalopathy* is the medical term for it, but you were not there, is the phrase I kept hearing.

My friend lived next to the World Trade Center and I was on the phone with her while she saw people jumping, close enough to see the color of their socks. Her husband urged her to move away from the window. Why are you doing that to yourself, he asked. She said

Someone has to watch them

She felt to walk away was to shut them out and so she stayed, holding them with her eyes and talking to them. It makes me wonder when they actually died. Don't we all wish they were dead before the asphalt rose to meet them with a force the human body should experience only in cartoons? That their hearts couldn't sustain that force and they died only after a rapturous feeling of flight? Did they have an in-between, or, like a cartoon, did their anguish and unsaid good-byes hang in the air like a cloud, invisible to anyone who saw their broken bodies on the concrete and had to look away?

I felt a partially opened window somewhere that might pull me through and this was not an abstract thought. I heard ugly words that I knew were bad news. They fell from the lips of your nurses with implicit underscoring: septic shock, hypoxemia, cyanosis. At one point there were at least nine people in my room and everyone was moving so fast. I became somewhat conscious and was asked questions about "proxy," and who to call "in case." I kept asking why I couldn't call someone myself? My phone is somewhere, I babbled. I had to sign permission for a procedure that could potentially puncture a lung. I heard the head nurse shout out "I'm doing this the old-fashioned way, don't talk to me about fever reduction, go get me fucking ice, I'm doing this myself." More faces filed through. One of your fellows said, "You will feel this," as he took a scalpel and sliced into my thigh to prepare a femoral cannulation. As he stitched me up I whispered, am I going to be okay? Speaking to himself more than me, he said

We are doing the best we can, I promise

Late the next day you came to my room. Everyone was required to wear masks and no one could touch me but a few of my friends were there. Yourself and a few colleagues were going to have a drink and celebrate that I'd made it. I saw my friend Nikki's face fall when you said that. It just kept getting more real, how gone I almost was.

I moved my oxygen mask to the side for a second but you motioned for me to put it back. "Where are you going?" I asked.

"Just a place down the street, it's called Parish."

I said, "Seriously? Could they not name it 'Thrive'?"

My friend Adam said, "No, dummy, he said, 'parish,' like a church," he turned to the doctor to make certain, "Right? With an 'a' not an 'e'?"

"Yes, yes! Oh God, sorry," you said, "definitely with an 'a,' not Perish!"

"Like clergy," said Hunter, as Joan, the evening nurse, entered. "Look at this, pure gold, that's what I'm talking about!" she said, holding up my catheter bag and giving a fist to the heavens.

"I mean, pure gold is definitely what comes to mind when I think of your urine," said Adam, his voice muffled through his mask, "and don't even start me on your sputum."

I got to watch people trying to save a life. I felt mine pulled away and back in spurts of protest and compliance. From a completely different vantage point I got to measure a length of mortality against that infinite question mark. Best of all, there is a small but distinct category of negative thought that I abandoned somewhere when I realized I only had the strength to hold so much and something had to go. I can't decide where existence lies or barely dangles, and Doctor, maybe you don't know either, but I can tell you I am humbled by the second chance. I don't know what death is, but I am one hundred percent clear on what it isn't.

It isn't my daughter refusing to try on a pair of shoes while the salesman admonishes me for buying her the wrong insoles and then leaving the store furious as my daughter says, "I want you to know I support you one hundred percent. Can today be the day I start on coffee?" It also isn't the dog digging a pack of gum out of my purse and chewing it, then peeing on the gum wrappers and crawling in my lap, making me forget to hate her. It isn't having the door handle to my office break off in my hand when I realize my only keys are in there and then remembering that, oh yeah, these are luxurious problems. It isn't having too much to do and wanting to scream and it isn't screaming. It might be poetry, but it isn't sitting and hearing it read by my son, it isn't him giving a standing ovation for the actor with the smallest part or my daughter confessing that she lied and then doing a cartwheel. It isn't getting a whole email in ESL from my niece and not caring that it's politically incorrect because I laugh so hard while reading it that I actually cry tears. It isn't *Antiques Roadshow* after sex for the sixth time while the sheets threaten to disintegrate. It isn't me listening to my children breathe at night and that being enough to want my heart to keep pumping blood. That one, mine, was not the only heart you saved. Sure they may have used the loss of their mother to fuel them in life toward a greater purpose. Or maybe it would have been so damaging that they'd never fully come back. Thanks to you I don't have to watch either of those scenarios play out while perched on a cloud fighting with God to let me intercede, or spend eternity aching to at least become the quivering sunbeam that lands on them one morning when they roll out of bed aged twenty-five.

As my friend Father Bob says, medicine can be more art than science. I believe the best doctors are a particular category of artist, with the creator's instinct to throw something on a canvas and start expanding, which must come down to divinity and the ability to judge what would bleed well into what.

It was too scary for me to face, my body giving me warnings of being so screamingly temporary. I wonder how often we are being nudged but we turn away. We find a place to jettison all of it, or hand it to someone and say, here, please organize this for me, I can't stand it. It would be eerie if those warnings lingered somewhere, the sound of them: *Run home, Don't answer the door, Walk away from him now*—What if that lasted?

If only I knew what "last" meant. "There is no now," my father would say, banging his cane on the floor on the word *now*. "As soon as you say the word, it's already in the past. When is it? There isn't one."

This is the only moment and it has already passed. The only things suspending time are children and cross-country travel. Not even all our stars are moving, that was light-years ago; it's only us here, dying as slowly as we can.

Dear Gorgeous,

I have won a prize. The prize comes with a cruise through our galaxy with a couple of stops on habitable planets. I am required to bring one man.

Our spaceship is stocked with oversized couches and fifty-foot-wide windows to view Earth from every angle. Spaceship has fine cheeses and rare wines that you recognize because you have an appetite for rare.

The man I am bringing is you, Gorgeous.

You are impossibly tall. Your tall intoxicates me. Your tall is nearly ridiculous. When I come back down from going on half-toe to kiss you, I yawn from the altitude adjustment. When you walk down a hall your head grazes the ceiling and you do a sweeping thing that isn't fey. It's as though you left your cape and crown at home to be kind. You left your scepter in a cab because you are absentminded yes, but really deep down you don't like to make others feel lesser.

Others are lesser.

You wave your hand through the air to dismiss something that displeases you and it's tantamount to another man firing a machine gun.

You do not need a machine gun.

You are so tall that if I'd ever lain underneath you (which is incomprehensible why I didn't) (though now I can since you're coming to the moon with me) (in my fantasy where we'll cruise our outer and inner spaces) I could have hidden there.

The spaceship will have your Pulitzer Prize that I will hold sometimes and pretend is mine. This will make you laugh. All your books are there also, and you'll read me your poems but it won't tire you. When you do sleep I'll hold your books to my face, mouth open; my inhalations dragging some of your genius into my lungs, ink dripping from the corners of my mouth. I'll exhale poetry onto paper afterward and when I read them aloud you'll say

I think that one is really promising

I'll kiss you and bring you a glass of wine. I'll tell you how handsome you are and how tall and kiss you deeply again and take off all your clothes. Your body will be forty years old, and then seventy years old, and then fifty. My body will be thirty-five years old, and seventy, and then we will end on our actual ages and decide reality is the way.

That will be the best moment but I am not at all spoiling it by telling you in advance. You'll see.

Dear Emergency Contact,

"Shut up. Get out!"

"I haven't seen it," I said.

"No way! Get out. I'm shutting off your morphine drip right now," you said.

"I haven't, I swear. Who's in that?"

"It's Bette Davis, and she, like. Oh my God. She basically gets sent to a sanitarium for having a unibrow." You laugh. I think at the memory of the brow.

"The unibrow made her unstable?"

"No, but at the beginning—I'm sorry I still can't believe you haven't seen *Now, Voyager!*—she has a unibrow and they send her away to a sanitarium. She doesn't have the brow at the end of the movie, and really nothing else was actually wrong with her? I mean, look, as soon as you get out of this hospital we're watching it."

"I want to see the brow," I say. I stand up slowly. "Should I walk? I think I should try to make it down the hall."

I take your arm and we walk to the end of the hospital wing. Today you have on light flannel trousers and a perfect white shirt. Even for a fashion designer you look sharp.

"It's chilly out here. Let's drape," you say, placing an extra hospital gown around my shoulders. I stand dutifully while you arrange it, tying the strings at an asymmetrical angle so that the gown falls off my shoulders like a pashmina. "No. It's too Opening Night at the Met. Wait." You take the gown and twist it, letting it fall around my neck in front with the ties falling down my back. "A cowl! But . . . it's a little Yohji Yamamoto for the hospital. Wait." You take it and hold it to your chest, considering.

"What about upside down?" I ask. The day nurse passes us and asks if she can change my bedding. "Sure, thanks," I say, putting a foot into the gown, which you are already holding up so I can step into the armholes, now upside down like a pair of shorts. The nurse eyes us. "Very creative," she says, nodding. "Hey, whatever it takes," you say. "And anything can be worn upside down. Look!" You size me up, pleased as I do my best at a catwalk strut. "Jumpsuit! Very Marisa Berenson circa 1973. If only it were in navy jersey with a floppy hat and chain belt."

You first put me in a dress when I was twenty-four or so. It was my first important dress, and I had no idea how to find an important dress or what it should look like. I mostly wore spandex and leather with combat boots, which is what I had on when I came into the store where you worked. You found me the perfect gown, taking it as seriously then, when I was not yet a friend, as you do twenty-five years and countless dresses later. Plenty of fancy people came into your store but you gave me the same attention. It's more important to you that a woman feels pretty than you getting credit for how she looks, but your creativity runs deep. More than once you've shown up with a stack of dresses and said, "I brought these, which you'll love, but. I had a vision. I dreamed you wore this," and you'll hold up whatever dazzling creation inspired you at three in the morning.

Snappy dresser, snappy with the snappy comeback, amidst all the snappy-ness it's easy to underestimate your humanity. Just so you know, I caught on. You donate your money and time when no one is looking, and are never remiss in sending a kind, handwritten note. Also, I saw the handbags you snuck to my daughter when you gave her a tour of your office. Busted. I have seen more than you probably realize.

I don't know how you knew to show up at the hospital when I was sick, but you sat with me more than once for an entire day. When you first got to me I was out of it. I was still quarantined and you stood there in a mask, holding a bunch of barrettes and headbands you'd brought me. The nurse came in again, asking for an emergency contact. She'd come back three times and I couldn't give her an answer. Family was too far, friends were busy and had their own kids, and I hated bothering someone in the middle of the night.

"Can I give it to you later?" I asked.

"Shut up. Put me," you said, waving her back in the room. "Seriously, shut it. What else am I doing at two in the morning? I'm the emergency contact," you karate chopped one hand into your other open hand on every syllable for effect, "end. of. sto. ry."

"But—" I started.

"But nothing. Listen. Seriously. E-nough."

I might have cried if I'd had the energy. Actually I probably cried a little, that day is blurry, but I do remember that and I know I can count on you, having called you at the eleventh hour and said, "Hey, I decided to go to the Emmys after all, can you make a dress?" or, "Hey I think I am getting married next Saturday do you still have that pink thing that I never wore?"

You are prepared and honest and you get there. After our little *Project Runway* jaunt down the hospital corridor I was exhausted and as you headed out I was already dipping in and out of sleep but I heard you in the hall with the nurse.

"She's done the vitals, the doctor said she doesn't need them again, and she had the other meds at nine, so let her sleep. Seriously, enough with the waking every two hours for no reason, let's give the woman a stretch of sleep, please."

"Are you her husband?" asked the nurse.

"Whatever, sure, friend, husband, just let her sleep."

I remembered the Christmas list I'd made in my mind a month before. Just dreaming up things I'd love to have, from whatever Santa might be dying to grant my personal wishes. In my head I took a pencil and happily crossed out one at the top:

5. ~~EMERGENCY CONTACT~~

Dear Future Man Who Loves My Daughter,

First of all, show up a bit late. It may be better if she's seen a little of the opposite of you, and relaxes in your arms only once she realizes you don't have a gruesome face hiding under the one you first showed her.

Do not have another face hiding. Yeah. I really would not.

Swoop in late, but not so late that she doesn't trust it when you say you want to make her drunk on happiness.

Make her drunk on happy.

Make her unhappy. Put yourself first. Do that awhile. Do it long enough so that she suffers. When she is done with that suffering, which will only make her more compassionate, watch as she rises up like the sea's last wave and crushes you with her silence. Notice how that silence moves in on you as she speaks, telling you that she's had enough and you have to change. You will see her mouth moving and recognize the words falling out and forming sentences that mean "Quit this moment or I will quit you," but the quiet that continues to threaten with staying forever if you don't comply? That is so much louder than her words. She will not be crying, or begging. She will realize she is powerful and perfect alone and that she doesn't need you. Her commitment to those words will terrify you. You will change for her because you realize no one is more worthy of changing for.

Remind her that she is beautiful in every new language you can invent. Careful with metaphor, as by then her mother's overuse of it may have exhausted her and made her immune to poetry.

Remind her about poetry.

If she has given you children remind yourself every day of the second, third, fourth, fifth, and sixth words in this sentence.

If you hurt her in ways that are irreparable I will send out people to hurt you back, sorry, but it has to be like that. Yes, you may have had a difficult childhood, but please allow me to introduce myself: Hello, I am the woman who doesn't give a shit.

Make her something warm to drink in the mornings and give her time to begin speaking; only rush at her with an embrace or a gemstone. Wildflowers. A love note. Yeats.

Do not fight with her in public. This almost includes the dog. She has an elegance that should not be polluted by compromising her privacy. This has something to do with loyalty, I am not sure how, but it does. Speak glowingly of her to everyone, even on the days she has infuriated you. Inflate! You have landed the loveliest girl walking the earth. Let too many people know how proud you are, so that it gets back to her and she feels proud to be herself.

Take her hand. Notice how like a piece of art that is.

Be a friend to her brother. Be a brother to him. Help him out if he needs it, and give him the opportunity to help you. Call him for no reason, and drop by with her on days you may not feel like it just to make sure they stay connected and trusting.

If her brother is telling a story about me in which I seem especially annoying, please feel free to poke fun. I want them to take comfort in the fact that they share a mother that is only theirs, and a childhood as wild and special as they are. I need them to have each other. It's almost all I need. My brothers have protected and championed me in ways that she will need also. Should someone slight her honor or threaten her, her brother will get into the ring and I hope you will join him. I have watched him do this already and it fills me with pride even when their fight is against me. My own brother came to the bus stop with me when he learned I wasn't getting a seat because of my rampant unpopularity. He stood there, arms folded as though he were barring everyone from entering the rest of their lives if they did not comply with his wish to treat me with respect. He said nothing but stared into the face of every kid on that street corner, promising that their futures were going to remain in question unless they understood. All conversation stopped. One person snuck a look at another and his head whipped around to catch both of them looking incredulously at one another in response to his threat.

Try me

his eyes said. And

Don't think I won't

The bus pulled up. I got in line and looked at him still standing there with barely contained galvanic ire. I tried to convey my thanks. His eyes said back

That's how much

I knew how much, but it was good to see it. Needless to say, I got a seat. I saw a different shade of that in my other brother the day my son was born and he came into the hospital and shuffled out all who did not belong so that I could rest. He took my son in his arms and read to him. He read *Winnie the Pooh*, the beginning of Ginsberg's "Howl," E. E. Cummings. He sang "New York, New York" as his first lullaby. Them together in that chair was one thing I will go back and watch if they let you do that at the end.

Make sure you know her uncles and her brother so well that she'd be jealous of your relationship if it didn't make her so happy. If she is in danger of forgetting her brother's birthday, remind her and when in doubt, invite him. To wherever. He is more important than you for her in most ways and I know you will understand. I agree that I'm asking a lot of you but remember

You already won the grand prize

Congratulations. Really. She is still in middle school now and insists she will never marry, but I am quietly hoping she and her brother both find something like my parents had, that endures and comforts them. Something lit by its own moon.

Be worthy of her. God bless you for noticing the right one.

Dear Oyster Picker,

Oh, but you have no idea.

Let's just say we were both in a hurry. That isn't presumptive of me. There's no way an oyster picker would survive in the Pacific Northwest if he were even a little bit slow. Most of you have been doing that hard job for years, but the men who start young become worn down while they're still pushing through their first acres of low tide.

Raw oysters are not cheap, but if you trace that pearly slip back to the moment it was plucked, you'll find an underpaid someone who did the plucking. Please, though, I'm not suggesting that you work a lowly job. I just mean that you should make at least as much as a gynecologist, who spends less time than you do all hunched over and plunging into the salty depths with rubber gloves on. You probably go through two pairs of those gloves a week, not only to shield you from the frigid surf but to guard against the gashes that end up on your wrists and forearms from those tongs that pry your crop from its seabed. Your back must ache from being bent over for hours while slogging through mud that can reach your knees. That tub of mollusks that will make memorable someone's first date can weigh up to seventy pounds. I suspect that costs your body a lot.

I wonder if you grow tired of always wearing the sea. Dragging the sound of waves to your pillow every night, you must fall there as light as an astronaut once your ankles are unshackled of wet earth and seaweed.

I've tried to imagine your face when I would tell you our story. The one about how we never met and how I have many pieces from you collected and sorted. I picture myself walking to you at the shoreline and waiting until you see me. I play that tape over and over with no sound, our voices drowned out by the unrelenting applause of the ocean. I tell you everything too emotional and abstract to say to someone you don't know, but still you understand it. You understand all of it.

When they came to collect my father's body my mother stayed in the apartment. Rather, she continued hovering there in a nonstate, so in shock and heartbroken as to not be included in the census count. Two men carried his body out the door on a stretcher while we four children followed down the hall. It was another moment of everyone trailing our father but this time he wasn't in front with his wool cap and cane. When we got onto the elevator and the door closed we each moved in closer to his body, now covered with a white sheet. Not looking at each other, we were at attention. All of us puffed up and unblinking; his parliament of owls keeping watch until we reached the garage where his body would be put somewhere to be driven somewhere else.

When they opened the doors to the back of the van my sister suddenly presented a photo, a large one I'd not seen her holding. In an inspired gesture of divinity she showed those two men my father's picture and said

This is who he was, so that you will know who you carry in that van, which is not just a body. You will know what we are leaving when we turn and go

She tried to complete a sentence that began with "He was—," but could not, and didn't have to. Her inability to finish that sentence and the flush that filled her face as she looked for words worthy of him were enough to finish it for the men, who understood. One of them reached to touch her arm. My brothers shook their hands after they looked at his picture, whispering acknowledgments to us that they would remember his face and thanking us for letting them see it. They were full of grace. It's hard to believe they'd ever removed a father's body before and left four adult children standing helplessly in a garage. They were so sensitive and respectful that if it was their fourth father of the day, they deserved some kind of medal.

When they started to close the doors of that van that would carry my father's body away, I knew part of him was in there still, in a plastic bag under a sheet. They were taking that away. I imagined hearing the van's doors closing, what that would sound like from the inside of a bag. The sound he would hear from the inside of that bag was too horrible and he was alone. He wouldn't know where they were taking him and worst of all, I explained as I tried to crawl and then stiffly force my way in the back of the van, worst of all I cried

my father is afraid of the dark
please don't make him go by himself
it's too dark in there
he will hate it

They pulled me away from his body. I kept trying to tell them I would be so quiet if they would please let me go too, but no one said yes and the doors closed. My sister tried to put her arms around me but I shoved her out of the way, not even the hurt on her face could bring me back as I ran after the van, I ran up the ramp and out into the cruel daylight. I was like a creature come from underground, it was too bright outside and the van drove purposefully, slowly through the parking lot just as you would while carrying a dead person, but I couldn't catch up. It turned onto the main road and I howled and begged it to come back until I just stopped and blocked my face from the sun with both hands. I sobbed from somewhere that owned me. I had no more will but to attend to those sobs. There was nowhere to go now. I had no clout with myself. I managed small steps but every direction was bad. There was nothing forward. I was fatherless to the right, with no one as my eternal champion, and fatherless to the left. I rotated in a broken waltz in that hateful sunlight which clearly had no idea what it would never shine on again. I turned help-lessly in my circle there on the only piece of earth that knew me without him, wailing in my hands and pivoting mechanically like the top of one of those music boxes he loved so much. Draining itself into dissonance until someone shuts the lid.

In photographs, the fog on the sound is so dense that it makes your workday plateau look like perpetual judgment day. Are you used to that? Do you ever look up and expect to see a spirit fly through the backdrop? Like my sister did in that mo-ment, I wish I could produce a picture of my father for you. I'd show you the one I have of him eating your oysters while my brother and I sat on the coffee table in front of him. Our faces in the picture are serene. We are giving our father exactly what he wanted and probably for the last time. Getting them to that TV tray, though, had felt tantamount to launching the shuttle. I suddenly understood that they weren't something you could just go and pick up.

I need to clarify for you exactly why I ran so hard to find them. Why I called everyone I could think of short of the Chamber of Commerce, and would have stopped at nothing to get a couple dozen oysters with whatever accompanying sauce. If you knew another part of the story, would you say I was acting out of habit? That I was still the little girl who felt it her position in life to shield her father from disappointment? That isn't the picture I want you to see.

My father was a soldier. I imagine you understand isolation. After the parades and champagne, men who came back from World War II had internal wars to fight on their own. My dad found a way to go forward, but returned to battle five years later during the Korean War. If there is even a point to distinguishing levels of Hell, the combat he faced in Korea was more ruinous. The conditions were horrific. Korea was preponderant chaos and carnage; being hit in the face with icy wind and the raw body parts of fellow soldiers were more visions to follow him home, and my mother woke in the night to the sound of him screaming while he relived them.

Though he was involved in the beginning of it, the Vietnam War was the end for him. He saw enough of a war he was opposed to and left the army before it was officially over. Almost forty-five years old and he'd survived three wars, been in and out of combat since the age of nineteen and the body bags from this war held soldiers not far from the age of his oldest son. He retired from the army and went to work as the manager of a bank. We moved to the suburbs with him hoping to always be home for dinner and never expected to hold a weapon again. Our house was the first I'd lived in not on an army base. We had a dog and a swing set, at the end of a cul-de-sac where kids rode their bikes and played statue at dusk.

An opportunity presented to be the justice of the peace for the county. He leapt at it, thinking a public service job would suit him better than the petty politics of the bank, but he soon discovered that this job had even more off-roads to corruption. After the army it became clear that he could not fit in with the world where accountability was something to get out of and rules there for bending. He refused to play politician and there was no elasticity in his morality. He didn't care who you were, there were no favors.

One of my brothers had a friend who sometimes stayed over for days. He was like a brilliant hippie version of Eddie Haskell and an accepted part of the family. One night when they were in their teens, this friend and my sister were driving in his VW Bug on their way to meet my brother when they saw the red lights of a police car behind them. He realized he had some contraband in the car and started to panic, telling my sister to get rid of it. She, ever compliant, started pitching the contents of the glove compartment out the window. Once she found his meager stash, she thought the best place to hide it would be her purse. Certainly no one would look in her pocketbook? Right about then the officer appeared at the side of the car to find the small mound she'd created: a still damp men's bathing suit, some Bob Dylan cassettes, and an empty Dairy Queen cup. He turned a flashlight on them, outshone by the beauty of my sister, who offered a winning smile while clutching her purse with white knuckles. He told them his intent was to inform them that they had a broken taillight, but he might need to have a look in that purse if she'd please hand it over. They were busted. It came to light that the lovely girl in the front seat was the daughter of the justice of the peace, and the tall long-haired boy a close friend. The officer knew that with two minors he was expected to bring the kids home. He was too savvy to roll up to the station with the daughter of the justice of the peace handcuffed in the back of a squad car, but still this was awkward. My father was playing cards with the chief of police at our dining room table when the doorbell rang. He answered the door and saw the officer there with both teenagers behind him. The policeman nervously explained the situation, and said he thought it best to bring them home to let my father handle it. He was going on while my dad stood quietly, squinting at him, and then he nodded and said, calmly

Yes, thank you. Book them

And shut the door on all of them.

Dad was called on regularly to pronounce people officially dead. The job of "county coroner" came with "city magistrate," and my mom recalls countless nights when the phone would ring and he'd sit up and sigh. He'd wearily go and stand over the mangled bodies of teenagers who'd crashed their cars driving drunk, or women stabbed to death by their husbands. The job was too much, and he was infuriated by the crookedness. He kept a log of people who offered him bribes, the paranoia and stress creating a pattern of him retreating in silence only to explode, usually at himself. A lower-profile job came up and he resigned, deeply relieved and optimistic for change. Sadly, this opportunity was tied to a contractor who held a grudge for a bribe not accepted. My dad's ethics had cost the contractor money, and this guy wanted revenge. He had Dad's new job cut without warning, and left him stranded. If he was out to punish my dad, he won.

My father was out of a job for two years. He grew bitter and paranoid, left with days that held nothing other than reading the paper and searching in vain for work. Too much time is a lethal trigger for veterans with PTSD, it can bring back the flavor of sitting in a foxhole and praying for daylight. There was nothing to distract him from a burning feeling of failure. Scrambling to provide for his family, he and my mother sold whatever they could to keep us afloat, they mortgaged and refinanced, maxed out every credit card. If his anger before was unpredictable, now it was pathological.

When he'd start I'd pull on his arm, pleading with him. "Don't yell, Daddy, please, I'm begging," I'd say. I'd put myself physically in front of him or take his hand and force him around to look at me. He'd sometimes stare past me in a kind of blackout, but if he heard me he'd come back to us like a sleepwalker who didn't know where he was. I'd see the confusion and shame wash over him, almost the worst part of it. The shame alone made him hate himself. It made him see white. We might get up mid-meal at a restaurant and leave with everyone staring while he shouted at someone. I'd redirect him back in the car if he pulled off the road to get out and bang on the hood, spewing profanity and putting each family member in a different state of shutdown. I'd coax him away from terrified shop owners while he was shouting or even physically lunging at someone. A chair would be thrown at the middle of the dining room table and glass would break, food flying. I'd hear one of the familiar refrains and grow hot in my face, feeling light-headed when I heard him say

I'm the goddamned son of a bitch

All right, so I'm nothing, I'm dirt to everyone

Maybe if I were dead it would be better

I knew that in an hour the house would be silent and my mother would be sitting at the kitchen table staring off, her long spidery fingers moving a water glass back and forth. My brother would be locked in his room listening to music.

When I was old enough to notice that the changing placement of paintings in our house were hiding holes he'd made with his fist, I knew to move them myself when someone forgot. I tried to make the present moment sparkle but I was never a natural ray of sunshine. I knew that what he fought was bigger than him but didn't understand that his distaste for the outdoors was the direct result of marching through inclement weather for days with an assault weapon in his hands while men were being shot dead in his periphery. I still don't know what he saw in his dreams that made him wake up screaming, I only know that I heard him and then I screamed too.

After those two years of waiting, he found another job but the same patterns repeated until he retired, stopped feeling obligated to impose his moral code on the world. He was tired now and welcomed the experience of having nowhere to go, nothing to police. He started to look at the world as a place he'd barely missed being wiped off of countless times. As the rage receded, his marriage became the focus. When my mother became briefly but gravely ill, it was as though someone shook him awake. I think his relief over not losing her helped him heal. One morning, late into his seventies, my mother remembered him being flip with her in front of a neighbor. Later on she saw him sitting staring out the window with one hand on his knee, looking unsteady. She said, "John, what's wrong?" and he said

Aw, hell, I feel like I wasn't respectful of your opinion. I hurt your feelings in front of someone else and that was wrong, I'm sorry

Their generation didn't quit on a marriage so easily, and they had a sacred love, private in a way that belied its obvious passion. It was only theirs. The tenderness in one glance was so intimate that you almost had to look away, even after sixty-four years together. More than one of his fellow soldiers would pull her aside after the war to tell her that yes, men had ways of coping but her husband was one of the only ones who never strayed. She would just blush when they told her how "you could ply him with booze and he would only go on about how he'd hit the jackpot with you." He was a flirt and loved women, but wouldn't tolerate or stay friends with a man who cheated. He said that sure, he understood temptation but didn't respect succumbing to it.

"Before I met your dad I had no idea that men like that actually existed," one friend said to me, and I heard that more than once. Those who met him in later years only knew him as unfailingly sweet and open, someone you could talk to about anything. Here was the man who found the interesting "fascinating," the amusing "hysterical," and the sad "heartbreaking." The rage from my childhood nearly vanished, and the positive, inclusive man was the one we could count on seeing when he opened his door. He was nearly healed but I meanwhile still had no idea what a normal level of emotion was in either direction. Was all that passed down? Did it soak into my subconscious, or was I born with it, a birthright? If terror creates adrenaline, does the fear just evaporate, the stain coming out in the wash? That cortisol was in his bloodstream. Meta-analysis shows that shock changes the size and structure of your brain, and I am half him.

The study of epigenetics says that the response to a traumatic event can be handed down as distinctly as the color of your eyes. Fear and rage can be ancestral. We love watching soldiers return home, their wives and children leaping into their arms with embraces and kisses that won't end. I myself have stood against a wall at the airport basically spying on a group of soldiers as they begin to deplane. I know those soldiers couldn't leave all that horror on the airplane, and some of what they had to bear may be handed down to their children. This isn't to take away from free will and all the heroic and damning aspects of accountability, it's just to suggest that genetic markers can't be wiped clean after traversing through Hell. If the science of heritability is correct you could be born afraid of things you've never seen and can't even name.

Near the end, when he was ill and all of us were on the couch next to him, telling jokes to cut the tension, my mother came in and put her hand on his shoulder, asked him if he needed anything, he said

Aw it just feels so good, to see them all sitting there together and laughing

He put a hand up to her face and lacking the strength to lift his face to her, he said

But you are the best medicine

My father took a level of pride in his children and grandchildren that was nearly freakish. The boys on my brother's football team thought my dad worked for the high school. They didn't know who that guy was who showed up at every scrimmage and every away game, even when it was snowing. He would stand there, staring at my brother, who left the bench just once when he intercepted a pass and then ran in the wrong direction, only to be tackled by his own teammate. He was crushed but shared such a good laugh with my dad that it seemed like his blunder was better than scoring the winning touchdown. He was back at the next game, never bored, in the same way that he was when he came to town to see me in a play for opening night. He'd shyly ask if it was possible to come back for the matinee, after which he would make it clear that if they needed help filling the house that evening, he was pretty sure he was available for that show, too. Birthdays were thought out months in advance. He'd pull me aside and say, look what I got your mother for Valentine's Day when it was not even Christmas. He didn't need a holiday as an excuse, though. My mother was heartbroken over the city tearing down her childhood home, where my father had picked her up for their first date. He drove over and dug, with his cane, through the refuse at the site until he found a brick representative of the house. He had the address carved into it and placed a picture of the house on top so she'd have something tangible to remember it by. He would sit around and think of things like that, what would make others happy, and then he actually did it.

When he first got sick he knew he had to tell us. My mother asked, what do I tell them and he said, tell them the truth, but

Damn, I just don't want this to upset their lives at all

He was very ill and I'd come in to help. We managed, after days of trying, to reach a monk in Mysore, India, who would give him a blessing. Daddy called himself an Episcopalian but was very interested in Eastern philosophy and Judaism, and open to most everything, really. Skyping with the monk, he grew so weak that he hunched over and rested his head on his cane while still attempting the chant of "om mani padme hung." The monk asked him how he was and he tried to pull himself upright, saying

Oh, I'm all right. How are you doing?

I got my father to his chair to rest. I decided to leave my parents' apartment for an hour and go to my hotel across the street. I walked toward the door and turned to him. "Anything, Daddy? Anything at all?" I asked. He caved in a little, collapsing on the idea of a wish being granted. He was not a man to ask for anything, or give himself much more than books, his one indulgence. Most requests to even get him a glass of water were met with, "No thanks, I'm driving." I saw him wrestling, and then realized I knew what that answer was. I knew before he said it. I felt like an ass for asking. If it had been a game show I would have won a car because he only managed to say

I don't suppose . . . I know it's too much to ask

when I held up my hand to stop him.
"No, no, I got it. I know what you want, Daddy," I said. I ran. I raced down the hall of my parents' apartment and out onto the

street. I kept running down the street to my hotel where I bolted to the elevator and made it up to my floor only to hit the button to go back to the lobby again, through which I barreled, back to the concierge just in case they had an idea, but they did not. The concierge could not find me raw oysters, could actually not find any oysters at all that night. They suggested getting frozen clams from the Piggly Wiggly on the interstate and thawing them in the microwave.

In the Pacific Northwest where you were it was not yet dawn. You were already busy wading through low tide. Was there ever a pride in knowing you were harvesting something rare? Like most things, I never wondered how it ended up in front of me until I couldn't find it. Maybe you were cursing us that morning, the people who would enjoy the result of the gashes on your arms and frostbite in your fingertips. Filling one bushel wouldn't grant you enough pay to buy a half dozen in one of those fancy bars. Despite his appreciating quality seafood, my father was far from fancy. If he'd been introduced to you I guarantee you he would have shaken your hand warmly and said, "John Parker, glad to meet you," and been actually glad. He would have listened to you with a soft and sincere chorus of "I'll be darned"s and "that's fascinating"s falling from his lips set in their crooked half-smile. His wide eyes with their bottomless dark would search yours, looking into you rather than at you, in the way of certain people who are always listening. Listening even when they are speaking.

He would carry our questions and problems into bed with him at night, truly considering them and aching to produce even a tiny solution. He'd call hours or days later and respectfully, he'd offer up

Hello, just your father. Correct me if I am wrong, but something occurred to me late last night

So yadda yadda Google, yellow pages, etc., gratuitous displays of emotion to strangers on the phone, my friend in New York City going on every food blog in the D.C. area; gross, shameless overuse of the phrase "beloved dying father," to messengers, restaurants, and caterers: groveling, offering, praying, and then, jackpot. The door to my parents' apartment opened that evening and my brother and I entered with bags containing clam chowder, corn bread, and one dozen each raw Blue Point and Olympian oysters; harvested by you, the hero of this book, wherever and whomever you are.

I now know, after saturating myself with info (the children forced to shuck them for thirty cents a day during the Industrial Revolution is another boo-boo in the arena of this experiment called homo sapiens and also, I don't know if you're aware of the illegal harvestings with a bunch of unlicensed pickers who ship contaminated crops to Britain?), about the harvesting of oysters. You, sir, would never have kept your job one day had you not been fast, nimble, and capable of withstanding enormous amounts of discomfort without complaining, quitting, or cheating. All of that makes you precisely like him, this man you'll never know. He went without plenty in his life, worked in coal mines and suffered on battlefields and in jungles. He was betrayed, abandoned, robbed, shot at, hit by a train twice, electrocuted, dropped from a plane with a faulty parachute (later meeting the rigger of said parachute in a bar and buying him a drink because "he was a nice fellow and he admitted it"), he was shunned and publicly humiliated for being a whistle-blower, went hungry and bankrupt, was left for dead, and survived brain and heart valve surgery. In spite of all that, by the end of his life he was the most grateful of men. His gift for receiving and for being appreciative was profound. The handwritten thank-yous he wrote were letters, not "notes," and he would go on for pages, describing how

the goodies arrived and I put the candy with my stash. I finished one book already, and the one on Buddhism, I can't put down. These gifts are a reflection of all the hard work on your part. We are so proud. Did you happen to get the last poem I sent?

and

If the Rolling Stones can tour at their age, we can too. Here I am in my hotel robe, in a room fully half the size of our house. I'm looking out at the Arno as the sun goes down, and oh, yes! Having a glass of champagne with your mother! It's almost too much to realize. You've made this such a memorable time in our lives. It just doesn't get any better than this

His fight to live honorably merited more rewards than I could dream up, but at the very least, he deserved those oysters. I swear he would have gone out there in waders and gloves himself if he'd been able to get up from his chair, but he couldn't, and this is why we needed you.

He gave as much of a smile as he could summon when he saw your oysters, he put his hand up and touched his white V-neck T-shirt and said

Be still my heart.

Aw, thank you, sweetie, will you look at that

I have the last white T-shirt that he wore in a bag inside another bag in my closet. I still haven't opened it, but I wonder if it carries the scent of your oysters, or the echo of one of his trademark two-note laughs that he let out when he looked at them on a plate before him. That little high-pitched giggle served as punctuation for just about anything, but usually one of his oft-used refrains: "That'll really take the wind out of your sails, *heh-hah!*" or, "Other than that, Mrs. Lincoln, how did you enjoy the play, *heh-hah.*" It was sometimes accompanied by serious eye-rolling but today he couldn't manage that.

My father went after your oysters with reverence. There was no show, just my brother and I watching him savor every bite with a stunning lack of ceremony. We gazed at him with complicit rapture, giving full respect to the experience you brought him. There was no after and no before.

I want to tell you now, that you who reached your bruised hands into the sea to bring my father his last meal: the shells you pried loose from the beds are in a bowl on my bookcase. I treat them like Fabergé eggs. I look at one up close and turn it over. I count them.

Because you got zero fanfare before, now you matter the most. Dearest Oyster Picker, you are like a change-of-life baby, showing up late and thereby cementing your position as favorite. You represent all of it, the men we never consider who slave for the safety and happiness of others, like my dad. It's man at his highest, don't you think? Besides, in looking for you I know so many terrifically cool things. I know how oysters help the environment by filtering ocean water and improving its quality like you can't believe. They provide a habitat for species of fish I had no idea existed, and help with nitrogen pollution by their consumption of phytoplanktons, whatever the heck those are, and I think help the quality of nearby bodies of water. Maybe. I'm not completely sure how they do that. Anyway I'm pretty sure they do, AND four oysters gives you a whole day's worth of copper, iodine, and some other thing. They are super-rich in vitamin B12, which is key if you are moody or have memory issues. The aphrodisiac component is sweet when you consider that oysters can and do change their gender midlife. Oysters are trannies! How can you not love them! It completely makes sense that Aphrodite chose to bust out of one, in her love goddess glory. Can you picture that moment with her springing up all ripe and golden, but out of a jellyfish? Or some algae platform? Oysters are so key and so fly that there is a whole movement to save them to keep their briny mojo working on the world. There are groups of hard-core oyster-lovers heading recycling projects, so the oyster never really dies. They plant new babies right on the old shells and send them back in. It's an easy way to contribute to Mother Earth and say sorry for all the hairspray and oil spills. You just drop them off at designated spots

and they take care of it. It's another thing I never considered before I considered you: Where did all those shells go? I just ate
them and forgot about it, as they became sky-high monuments to
hot sex and burgeoning zinc levels. All that landfill that could have
been going back home with a fresh start on a shell so happy to be
reincarnated.

I know you don't have time to do the recycling part but here's
the thing: *we can do it for you.* I've been looking at your shells in
the bowl and I'm going to find one that is giving me signals and
I'll send it back for both of us. I know how important your job is
now and I don't really forget those kinds of things once I learn
them. It's a tiny something I can do for you.

I will tell you now, Oyster Picker, the night after he had your
oysters he stopped speaking. Everyone went to sleep except me
and I sat next to him holding his hand. The last thing he said to
me was, he said

Squeeze my hand, please

I held it until that last breath flew out and he went wherever
it was he'd found where he wouldn't be scared or lonely for us.
Where he could continue on with the things you and I don't know
about yet.

When I heard from his doctor that he would die in a matter of
months or even weeks, I called him. I tried to talk both of us out
of it altogether. I knew he was afraid and I tried to say all this stuff
about, I don't know. It sounds so inane now. All the usual stuff
about how no one really knows anything, and he had every reason to stay open to miracles. We didn't know for sure what would

happen, I kept saying, and he said, yes, you're right. Then because he was the wizard of all fathers he asked me what I was doing, like that should have mattered. I said well, okay, I'm standing in this really awesome bookstore. You'd love it, I said. He gave a sigh of longing and said, oh my, tell me, they have anything interesting? I said yeah, tons. I'll send you a book from here, how does that sound. He said that's wonderful, that's just tremendous, thank you sweetie. I told him I was sending him some candy too and he thanked me, said he'd be on the lookout for it, and he then said, tell me, what are you writing now? You working on anything? I said oh Daddy, just little things, I don't know, and he said okay, but listen to me

just write, keep writing, promise me that you will.

Acknowledgments

First and hearty thanks to Scott Henderson for the constant encouragement and for leading me to the brilliant Eric Simonoff. (Eric, you are a giant.) Without him there would be no book. Humble thanks to Colin Harrison and Nan Graham at Scribner for their enthusiasm about this project and confidence in me; I am so grateful. For help and support: Debra Kletter, Larissa Laskin, Nicole Gillingham, Claudia Ballard, Nicole Burdette, Jake Honig, Frandy Rubio (you too, Andy), Amanda Hosten St. Louis, Katrina Diaz, Kate Barry, K. Todd Freeman, Josh Ritter, Hunter Parrish, Joe Morra, and Kirsten Parker. Peter Hedges, for help with the birthing of babies and books (and for Lucas). Deep bows to those who said that I could and should write: Craig Lucas, Mike Nichols, Mark Strand, Eli Attie, Mary Foote, Elizabeth Cuthrell, Merri Biechler, Jessica Lamendella, Dava Waite, Mary Karr, the chief himself, David Granger, Ryan D'Agostino, and everyone else at *Esquire*. For keeping it real and surreal, that's you, **DONKEY**, okay? Gratitude from **MY HEART'S DEPTHS** to my siblings Jay, Sage, and Bruce. My thanks is **FOR REAL LIFE**, especially to and for my two **ETERNALS**, my son, my daughter. To them, **ETERNALLY.**

About the Author

Mary-Louise Parker is a Tony, Emmy, Obie, and Golden Globe Award—winning actress. Her writing has appeared in *Esquire*, *The Riveter*, *Bust*, and *Bullett*. This is her first book.